W9-BFP-166

MOONBEAM IN MY POCKET

Seaburn

Ed Eriksson

Moonbeam In My Pocket
Copyright © 2010 by Ed Eriksson
All Rights Reserved including the right of
Reproduction in whole or in part.
For permission please write to the publisher:

Seaburn
PO Box 2085
Astoria NY 11102
www.seaburn.com

ISBN: 1-59232-247-6

Library of Congress Cat. Num.-in-Pub.-Data

2008 Eriksson, E.
Moonbeam In My Pocket

Ref. CSO.03S10-Sta2

As a work of historical fiction, "Moonbeam in My Pocket" is
purely imaginary. While names and places are used for
historical verisimilitude, the people in the novel are not real and
not meant to be a commentary on anyone living or dead.

Printed in the United States of America

MOONBEAM IN MY POCKET

Ed Eriksson

CHAPTER ONE

"Stealing Home"

I was called Moonbeam and still am. When I first joined the team I was so fast I stole three bases on opening day. When Toby Hughes, the Bluebird manager, asked me how I did that, I answered that I had a moonbeam in my pocket and whenever I went into second or third I could flash that moonbeam into the fielder's eye and slide under his tag. That wasn't true, of course, but I was young then, and I had a rich imagination. Even though I'd come from Baltimore and been to college for three semesters at Morgan State, Toby figured I was a fool black boy from a Mississippi tar shack who believed in a lot of nonsense. As a joke he related my explanation to the first base coach Franklin Byrd, and he told everyone else. By the next game I'd become Moonbeam to one and all, even though everybody knew that my rightful name was Carl.

By coincidence of birth my last name is Slyder. I've noticed that some people are born with names that say something about them. For instance, there was Billy Dublin, who played for the Grays and hit more doubles than anyone I can remember. There was Pretty Boy Handy, who played shortstop for the Kansas City Monarchs in the 1930s. He was handy, see, with ground balls, picking them up from anywhere between second and third and tossing out the fastest runners. Then there was Herman Glove, the catcher on my team, the Jersey City Bluebirds, who never let a ball get by him and who never smiled at me for the reason that he'd never stolen a base and never could, in any practice game, throw me out when I did. Oh, yes, there was Franklin Byrd, that bald and baggy-eyed coach, whose face always got a laugh, because he'd be one blue Byrd whenever we lost, and we'd lost a lot the first half of that '46 season.

The name I most remember in this way was that of Buster Fenton. This Buster was twenty-two when he came to us in late June, from Philadelphia, though he wouldn't speak about his hometown, being strangely reserved, even after a few glasses of beer. He would never tell anyone where he played ball before, giving the impression that he was a natural phenomenon come from nowhere. But, as I found out later, he'd been to Howard University and played college ball for a season. The word was that Uriah Holding, the Bluebird owner, saw him hit a few home runs at an exhibition game in Eaton, Pennsylvania and figured, what the hell, the team couldn't do any worse, why not put him in the line-up? Our record was 8-and-17: so maybe, it seemed, Mr. Holding was acting from desperation. As it happened, this desperation became inspiration, things turned out so well at first. And then they didn't, since the end, which came on fast, was so unlike the beginning.

Buster was a big-boned, handsome fellow, on the style, you might say, of Paul Robeson: about six-foot-two, with broad shoulders and strong lines to his jaw, nose, and forehead. He had dark brown naturally wavy hair. The rumor was that he had a white daddy; but I met his father: it was not the case. He was the sort of fellow you could get jealous about if you thought your girlfriend found him interesting. But, fact was, wherever we went, this Buster was well-behaved, keeping his distance from women as well as men. There was that air about him that he was not common. Oh, he would go out with us after a game and down a few beers, but that was all. By eight o'clock he was back in his room, reading a book or listening to a radio program. Herman Glove, his roommate, always defended him, claiming that we'd read about Buster some day in the history of the Negro race. "Let him be his quiet self," Herman would say, "he's going to do things rather than talk his way through life." Herman would give the impression that he had the real dope on Buster. That was Herman's way, acting superior, especially in matters of racial progress. However, Buster had no need to act in that sense. He had class. We all commented on it. When he spoke, it was low-keyed; his words were well-chosen; and he kept up his guard, rarely joking with anyone and never offending. So at first we had to rely on Herman Glove for tidbits of facts on Buster; and this we could do once we got him drinking. He would start laughing quietly to himself and then get that sly look in his eye and begin to spill the beans. He had that other side to him.

Our luck changed once Buster joined the team, because as a switch-hitter he could whack a baseball like nobody I'd ever seen, except, of course, Josh Gibson. But he was as powerful as Josh, batting right and left-handed; and if he'd lived he'd've been written down in all the books about the Negro Leagues--I began to believe along with Glove that Buster, in his way, was historic material--just like Josh. Yes, sir, we'd be hearing about him in the future, I thought. But that was not to be. Even so, he could slam home runs that sailed over the grandstands at five hundred feet! He could hit so hard that one summer afternoon he cracked the wooden railing in Cleveland's League Park, on a line drive at the three hundred and thirty-foot mark in left field! Splinters from that shot flew all over the grandstand. That's when I realized that he too had a name that spelled his destiny: for our Buster Fenton was a buster of fences! How do you like that? To be perfect, he only needed to change that "t" in Fenton to an "s." A small matter. Yet nobody knows his name now except me and two other fellows on the team; the ones still alive, I mean, and that would be the third baseman Steve Sylvester and our left-handed pitcher (a country boy if there ever was one) Boondocks Cooney; both, like myself, now in their eighties. Buster's photo appeared in the Negro newspaper in Jersey City a few times, once in a sensational way in "The Amsterdam News," the big New York City publication, and maybe elsewhere in Pittsburgh, Chicago, or Kansas City. But it was never, to my knowledge, saved in any sports archive. No, he came up fast and went down quickly. That's why I shake my head when I talk about him now.

Buster hit seventeen home runs in July of '46. By August our record was a neat 20-and-20, which means that with Buster batting third or fourth we'd won twelve games and lost only three: he averaging nearly two home runs a game!

My favorite of these shots came on the last day of a hot July in Kansas City, in baseball action that brought me fame for a little while. That game was a doozy, because when the ninth inning rolled around we were losing 6-to-3. You don't usually have a lefty as a lead-off hitter, but my speed earned me that place. Now, here I was for my fourth at-bat, starting the Bluebirds' line-up in the top of the ninth inning. I sauntered to the plate reluctantly, actually dragging my bat in the dirt. On the mound was the immortal Satchel Paige, who had struck out sixteen batters that day, including me twice. He was fast and unhittable. So imagine my surprise when he threw me an easy curve that came right into my zone, medium-high and slightly outside. I figured he would try and strike me out on three fastballs low and inside; but, no, Satchel was so self-confident he thought he'd have some fun with the Bluebirds, as a way to end the game. I considered, then, that he wanted me to hit for a single. Why? Because Satchel was a man so in control of his game that he proposed to tease us into defeat. On the next pitch, one exactly like the first, I swung and slapped a gentle line-drive over the shortstop's head and jogged happily to first base, proud to have singled off the incomparable Mr. Paige-- knowing all the time he'd given me the hit!

Once I stood on first base, the psychology between Satchel and me shifted, I supposed, in my direction, because now it became my turn to tease him. I suspected that he let me single so that he might catch me trying to steal second with some kind of hidden ball trick: he supposing, as well, that I'd run on the first pitch to the next batter. So I planned to test him through nine or ten throws to first base. Something like that. Satchel, I soon discovered, had set me up for another piece of business, I being part of a larger humiliation for the entire team. Very quickly he walked Henry Scoppits on four pitches; and I took second as Henry went to first. He did the same with Russell Coates; and all I had to do was walk to third and the bases were full.

I realized then what ol' Satch was up to. The fourth batter would be Buster Fenton--and Satchel intended to strike him out with bases loaded, Buster representing the winning run at the plate. This would show the younger slugger how much the older pitcher was his superior. Then, of course, the great one on the mound would strike out the next two batters, Curly Strong and Jock Renfroe. This would shame the Bluebirds before his, Satchel's, hometown fans along with giving him a new record, I think, for strikeouts--nineteen. (I think Satchel always had numbers running in his head.) But, beyond any consideration of team and victory, Buster was his reason for this playfulness. From him, I understood, Satchel wanted revenge.

You see, when Buster faced him for the first time on the July 4th double-header in Jersey City, Satchel underrated him as a young and overconfident big-boned nobody. Cockily, he wound up with that high kick of his and tossed a fast one down the middle--that the rookie blasted over the right field stands and out of the ballpark! It was probably the longest-hit home run off Paige in his career. If it didn't travel five hundred feet, it went pretty close to it. The people in the stands all stood and said, "Oooh!" in one voice. That would be one reaction a proud guy like Satchel would never forget. But the man only watched the ball with a slight turn of his head, standing tall on the mound, showing no sign of dismay. All I could read on him was a compression of his lips and a blowing out of air. He touched both sides of his pencil-thin mustache and went back to pitching his game. I suspect, though, he stored a need for revenge; and now some four weeks later he would get it. So he hoped.

That was what I surmised now that he'd walked Coates. There we were--Coates on first, Scoppits on second, me on third. And here came Buster Fenton, with his broad chest expanding and his bat hanging in his right hand by his side. He limbered up slowly, deliberately, on the right-hand side of the plate (that is, for a left-handed batter), swinging the bat in a high arc like a golf club, first with his right arm, then with his left. He stepped into the batter's box and settled his legs in wide, leaning a bit over the plate with the bat a few inches above his left shoulder. I still remember the easy power of his stance.

Kansas City is hot and muggy in the summer; it was around ninety-five degrees in Municipal Stadium that day late in July. By the ninth inning the fans had begun to leave, defeated by the heat. But once I singled, the movement in the stands settled into the slow waving of gray felt and yellow straw hats. I saw a lot of short sleeve white shirts all sweated through: The air was almost blurry with humidity; the green grass of the outfield had a yellow glow. Standing on third, I figured that Satchel must be getting hot and tired in spite of his inclination to shenanigans; he'd pitched the whole game. So I thought I might try something after all, such as bring attention to myself and away from Buster, giving the boy a fighting chance. I began to act hot and tired, removing my cap and wiping my forehead with my forearm. "Whew," I said out loud, "it is one damned scorcher!" Then I shuffled slowly off base, perhaps five feet, moving heavily as if I couldn't bear my own weight--no, sir, there'd be no running for me, just slogging.

Satchel was trying the same thing on Buster; trying, see, to seem weary so that the batter wouldn't expect anything but an easy pitch with maybe a little curve. Long-legged Satch bent down lazily for the rosin bag; straightened up and squeezed it, then dropped it; wiped his brow; shook his head; then leaned into his wind-up. He rocked back easily, kicked medium-high and then forward, letting go a pitch at about eighty-five miles an hour. A smooth, surprising pitch: it went the distance from mound to catcher's mitt as if riding on a fast, steady train. And of course that white thing went smartly by Buster, who just looked. Strike one.

Buster wiped his eyes, astonished at his own paralysis. Then he rubbed his face hard; he shook the daze from his head; and he gave Satchel his version of a surprise. He stepped across the plate and assumed a right-handed batting stance!

The Monarch's catcher, Jesse Rogers, looked back at the umpire, who shrugged and indicated for him to get ready for the next pitch. Naturally, even Satchel had to pay attention: Once so smug about putting that fastball past Buster, he stood there, puzzled, re-thinking his next pitch. He thought so deeply he didn't see me creep down the base path another five feet. Then getting self-conscious about dealing with Buster's unforeseen tactic, he turned his back to the plate to hide his face when he picked up the rosin bag. That is when time in the liquid-like heat of the day stood still for five seconds. You could've photographed Satchel in twilight with an old slow-shutter camera, he bent so slowly and held there, motionless. In that moment I broke for the plate.

Before Satch could drop the rosin bag I'd gone another twenty feet, running as if my heels glided on an incoming tide. I traveled so fast I lost my hat; I also lost sight of the man on the mound; I didn't see the catcher, much less the umpire; I saw only a piece of white plate, smeared with dirt between Buster's black spiked shoes; I felt only the cool wind of my speed. And then I slid.

Surprise is a great provider. Paige did not have the leisure to wind up and aim the ball. He had to throw sidearm, hurriedly. Consequently, his throw came off the plate towards first. As for the catcher, that large, chunky Jesse Rogers, he was unaware I'd advanced so close to home, and that's because Buster's right-handed batting position blocked his view of the third-base line. Moreover, when Buster saw me flying at him he didn't budge until I started to dip into a slide; then he pulled himself back and let me in.

As I slid, Jesse had to reach in the opposite direction to grab the ball, then swing his glove hand back again to make the tag--a hard play to make because you tend to lose your sense of distance in the movement. At times like these my moonbeam worked best; for I really did have one, though not as I explained to Toby on my first day or anyone after. That would've ruined the effect. So here is this big, awkward Jesse Rogers reaching for me with the ball in his mitt and his left eye, looking through his catcher's mask, gauging the position of my feet. That is when I flashed my smile: my Uncle Louis, my mother's brother, commented that I had the biggest, widest, white-toothed, pink-gummed colored mouth he'd ever hope to see--and it was that white-toothed grin that caught Rogers by surprise (his third surprise in three seconds, after Satchel's throw and my dash down the baseline). He jerked his head back a bit and misjudged the position of my feet as his glove came too high to make the tag. Actually, he touched my left knee, but my right foot, sliding below it, had just skimmed across home plate. Safe.

As I went back up the line to pick up my hat, I flashed another smile at Mr. Paige. The great one wouldn't give me any satisfaction: He inspected the stitching on his glove, refusing to glance back as I jogged off to the dugout. But I knew that I'd gotten him good, so much so that his plan of humiliating the Bluebirds was about to backfire entirely. In spite of his calm exterior, Satchel's brain was so agitated by my success--as the stands went wild with commotion, and this was KC, the Monarchs' home town--that he lost track of his agenda for Buster Fenton. He threw one more pitch to the rookie, who whacked it over the left field fence, giving us a 7-to-6 lead. Which we didn't give up in the bottom of the ninth; and so we won.

Now, I don't mean to brag. I say this for the record, though, that I am the only man ever to steal home plate on Satchel Paige. I think I am also one of the few men who caused his ego to wobble a bit--I say, wobble because I imagine a person's ego to be like a helping of jello that wobbles when disturbed: You may choose the color. For ol' Satch would never admit that I had stolen home that day. He claimed that we scored a run on his catcher's, Jesse Rogers', error! Now, I ask you. And the funny thing about all that was that no one kept a scorecard that day, that hot Sunday in July! So there is no permanent record now, only my claim. My glory lasted for a while in a buzz around the league and then disappeared into thin air. I should mention also that Satchel would never agree with Franklin Byrd that I was in fact faster, faster that '46 season, than Cool Papa Bell. But the proof of this judgment is that Mr. Paige never pitched easy to me again and never smiled back when I came to bat. It was almost as if he knew my secret.

I will say this for Satchel. He helped me off the field once when I didn't expect he would. But that's for later.

Enough about him. Back to me. I hurt my ankle that summer, running and twisting it too hard off the field, twice.

These events happened during moments of great desperation that grew out of the Buster Fenton Case and my involvement in it. There were no broken bones, just a sprain that didn't heal right. That's why I became a coach and then manager of the Bluebirds for their last half-season. Soon enough, you'll hear about that too.

Buster and me, we were braided together in a strange, tragic destiny. I believe my attachment to him began that day when I saw through Satchel's plan to humiliate the Bluebirds and saw, as well, a way to save Buster from the shame of that defeat. For, truth be told, I set that kid up to get the better of Mr. Paige. I knew that Satchel would strike him out if I didn't act to upset the pitcher's rhythm: Buster's switch-hitting at the plate would not be enough. And what would accomplish this object better than my dashing down the third-base line at the perfect moment? Of course, opportune moments don't come along every day; often you have to make them for yourself. This is what I did that steamy day in July. I did it for Buster and for the team. It's so much more rewarding at times when you risk for more than just yourself.

I'm not sure that Buster ever understood my original intention when I came sliding in to score. What he believed was that my steal came from his tactic of batting right-handed against Paige, since his move around the plate disturbed the pitcher's concentration. Plus, the heat was oppressive, and everyone was wilted. Everyone but Buster. Hitting a home run at that moment, well, how could anyone but you be the hero? After the game, the kid became more relaxed, even agreeing to meet me later and have one or two glasses of beer at The Golden Pharaoh Private Sports Club in the 18th and Vine, that is, the colored section of Kansas City--not far from the location of the Negro Leagues Baseball Museum that I have been connected with in recent years. This private sports club was a saloon where the players would wind down after a game, shooting pool, getting drunk, fighting, and playing pranks on one another. There were some easy women there, I should point out; but Buster was not one for getting drunk, joining in on the gags, or making friends with stray kittens, you might say. He had a classy fiancée in Philadelphia, he told me, describing her at length; and he didn't go in for pouring whisky down his throat, one shot after another. Neither did I. But a few of the boys were something else.

So after our victory we sat in this former colored speakeasy, now a private drinking club, where he agreed to meet me after the game. It was noisy with shouts and laughter and the click-clack of pool balls. We drank our beer and laughed a bit, at Satchel Paige specifically, since for once the joke was on him. We talked about when Satch was in his prime and struck out the mighty Josh Gibson with two outs and the bases loaded--and no one in the outfield! The great one had called all three outfielders in and then demolished his rival for fame, the black Babe Ruth, in three pitches, two looking and one swinging. We talked of how Josh was dying, as some said, of a broken heart for not having a chance to play in the Major Leagues. But most of us knew that Josh drank like no other man alive, and I believe all those post-game festivities, as much as anything, finally brought him down the following year. End of the road at thirty-five! By contrast, we spoke of how Satchel, who was now at least in his mid-forties, about the same age as the century, made more money than ever, barnstorming with white players like Bob Feller and Stan Musial; and how he would probably achieve what Josh never could, which is a contract with the white majors. Maybe the first man out of the Negro League and into the big time--well, either first or second, given that Jackie Robinson, who'd come out of nowhere, was getting a lot of publicity in this respect. I remember Buster's comment.

"Not first or second, not Satchel," he said. "He's too old; he's not the man he was."

His knowingness annoyed me. "Don't be too sure," I replied. "But that Robinson guy, he played a bit for the Monarchs here last year; and now he's signed with the Dodgers. He's up in Montreal, playing for their farm team. He'll be first; then Satchel."

"Then me," said Buster, nodding. "Ever see that eventuality?" He cocked his head to the side with a thin, secret smile. That home run today, I thought, has gone to his head. But he knew more than I did then. He raised his eyebrows and sipped his beer. Leaning back in his chair, he glanced off to the corner of the ceiling--yeah, he knew something nobody else on the team did. "I think I can do it," he smiled again, looking back at me, "If I want to."

If he wanted to? Did anyone know his name? Any Major League owner? Any baseball scout? Anyone beyond the team's management and players and his Philadelphia fiancée?

"If only there were one rich white cat in the ballpark today," I said.

"There were a few," he answered, a bit mysteriously.

"So you say." But I admitted I'd seen someone who looked like a Major League scout and, oh, yeah, Tom Baird, the Monarchs' chief owner, sitting up behind our dugout with another fellow, a strange guy, actually, who stared at me with sad, dark eyes. Not much else in the way of whiteness and money.

"Stared at me too," he said, frowning, getting thoughtful and detached, as if I weren't there.

Since I'd have to spend more time pondering what his mood meant, I decided to change the subject.

"I saw what you did today," I offered, referring to his move in the batter's box and his blocking me from Jesse Rogers' view. I expected him to compliment me in return; but he didn't; he'd gotten a serious look on his face, and I realized he was too absorbed in his own potential--and some dilemma that potential posed to him--that he didn't see anyone but himself as critical to his success. He may have comprehended how I upset Satchel Paige's plan for him; but next to his three-run blast my stealing home was minor. And so, considering his youth and his strange brooding expression, I let it pass.

"Everyone saw me," he said, and that "everyone" had a curious ring.

"Everyone," I echoed flatly.

"You're a nice guy, Moonbeam, a gentleman," he said, smiling as he sipped his beer. "Here," he suddenly added.

From his equipment bag he produced a long, narrow rectangular box. "This is not for you," he explained, placing it on the table. "It's for Jamesetta Kelly, my fiancée. But I want you to keep it for me. To give to her. If something funny happens. To me." He spoke deliberately. "Okay?" I nodded okay. After asking the barmaid for pencil and paper, he wrote down Miss Kelly's address and slipped it into the box. He finished by imploring me to keep this business to myself. I nodded again. When I asked him if I could see the contents of the box, he lifted the lid and showed me a glass rose, with red petals, green stem, and two green leaves. He said nothing, and I simply stared at it until he closed the box and pushed it towards me. Oddly, then, he began to praise the girl in glowing terms: She was an ideal but a fragile one, he noted, so if I ever had occasion to meet her, I should treat her gently. Then he grew silent; he turned away and let his eyes roam all around the saloon.

I hoped he might explain further, perhaps after another beer. I mean, what had he to worry about? When he turned back to me, he had that self-pleased expression, as a person has when he is about to tell a joke. I supposed that maybe now I could reach into his heart and discover his secret, for secret he had beyond his idolizing this Jamesetta Kelly, and it was one with an unspoken dilemma.

"So," I began after putting the white box into my equipment bag, "is Buster your baptismal name?"

But at that moment a sudden ruckus started at the other side of the barroom, some louder shouting and some shoving. I stood up to catch the action. Apparently, Boondocks Cooney, our left-handed pitcher, was in the center of it, as was often the case. This troubled me because Boondocks was pretty stupid, for that is how he got his name, and he wasn't able to defend himself except by swinging his fists. He came from Alabama, and he could throw a baseball like a demon; but he could barely execute a double play on a ground ball: He couldn't remember, see, to throw to second when a dribbler came to the mound. "Just jump down and turn around," they told him; "you know, like the song says: 'Jump down, turn around, pick a bale of cotton?' See?" He didn't see it. So the joke was that he became a ballplayer because he was too inadequate to pick cotton. Those cotton-picking taunts were endless. He used to laugh at first at this ridicule; then he got wise all of sudden and hit Steve Sylvester with a left hook that knocked out a tooth. These days all you had to do to get him going was let him hear the words "Boon the Coon" from the other end of the bar; and this, I suspect, is what happened that evening.

As I moved into the fray, trying to think of a way to bust it up, I heard the band strike some dramatic chords. Soon the singer, fat and happy Alona Mae Driscoll, came to the microphone and hummed a few melodious notes. The drummer crashed into his percussion set, sounding the cymbals and the bass drum hard; and everyone calmed down and looked towards the bandstand. Getting serious, Alona Mae wailed her way into a favorite blues number, going, "Oooh ah, oooh ah, oooh ah" and then huskily sang the words:

> Sorry, sorry, my heart,
> We been together so long,
> And now we got to part,
> Oooh ah, oooh ah, oooh ah,
> Sorry, so sorry, my heart.

So the fight broke up and the saloon got quiet again. I happened to look down at Buster, only to see that he'd disappeared, leaving half his beer undrunk. I turned towards the door, and, yep, there he was, duffle bag on his back, easing his way past two young lovelies who wanted to grab and cling to him with their little kitteny claws. In a flash he caught my eye and then saluted me by touching his forehead with a slight wave. Once free of the girls, he was through the door and gone.

Was he going back to the boarding house to read a book? Man, was he aloof. Surely, he would have helped me pull Boondocks out of the scuffle. He wasn't afraid to get his hands dirty, I don't believe. But why turn his back on Alona Mae, the Kansas City Torch?

> You never understood my pain;
> And, it's true, I always laughed at yours:

Oh, yeah, oh, yeah, you take that midnight
train,
Oooh ah, oooh ah, oooh ah,
Oh, yeah, oh, yeah, you take that midnight
train,
'Cause you never understood my pain,
And I can't help laughing at yours.

The music had the power to distract everyone except Buster. After the song, everyone went back to laughing and drinking. Things got quiet again as Alona Mae sang a few more times. I sat and had another refill. But I wasn't listening. There was some silly stuff with Franklin Byrd's fixing out a device to drench second string infielder Alonzo Emmett with a pitcher of beer, a thing that tipped over his head above the door to the men's room. But soon I got up and returned to Mabel Hamm's boarding house where six of us roomed. There was myself and Curly Strong; Steve Sylvester and the outfielder Jock Renfroe; and then Herman Glove and Buster.

I hit the pillow and fell asleep around eleven o'clock. Abruptly, some time later, I was awakened by Glove, who'd come to the room to wake me, so he said; and when I didn't respond he'd leaned over the bed and jostled me--then backed discreetly into the doorway.

"Where's Buster?" he wanted to know. He repeated the question as I came to a sitting position, just opening my eyes and seeing him framed into a silhouette by the hall light behind him: He looked dark and ominous.

"He's in your room, man," I said. "Curly's in here with me."

"Nobody's in there with you."

"Nobody?" I checked the other bed. No Curly. Empty.

"Maybe they're still out, in some bar or other," I couldn't focus just yet. "You know how it is."

"Curly, maybe," said Herman, whispering loudly. "But that kid, he's no drinker. He's no company for Curly. He's in bed every night at ten."

17

"Yeah, so?"

"Something's wrong. The kid should be in bed."

Glove was like that, everything needing to be the way it ought to be.

"Kid's over twenty-one," I said, sitting by the bedside in my underwear. "I'm no chaperone." I was rubbing my eyes, hoping he'd go away. But then I knew he was right. Something was wrong. "Are you his good angel?" I asked. Herman stood still, looming there like a phantom of rebuke: stocky Herman, oblivious to my sarcasm, expecting me to do the right thing. "I'm no chaperone," I repeated.

Like a zombie, though, I rose and dressed. Herman and I went tippy-toe out of the boarding house, heading for those dark, lonely streets with the upstairs lights on; I mean the red light district of Kansas City; where we might meet some other teammates and perhaps Buster Fenton. Who knows what secret pleasures call a man to do what he does in the dark?

It was two a. m. when we left the boarding house. We must've traveled for the next two hours, up and down the streets, in and out of houses and ramshackle hotels and sleepy, dim-lit saloons. Our sense was that Buster would get himself in trouble, either with some gal or some pimp, and not knowing much of the town would wind up bruised or cut or worse. He'd left The Golden Pharaoh early. How much time would he have required with a two-dollar-a-night floozy?

We saw no one we knew, except for David Lincoln Jones, the sportswriter on "The Kansas City Afro-American," a gentleman with gray hair and natty clothes, worn awkwardly. His bow tie hung untied from his unbuttoned collar; his jacket was wrinkled, his slacks soiled; and he was drunk as a loon. Overjoyed at meeting us, he promised to write us up big in this week's issue. "And that high-falutin' college kid," he was saying, "that ten-cent Jackie Robinson, that bleached out Josh Gibson; that, that, well, you know who I mean." He meant Buster, we supposed, and supposing that we also supposed he'd run into him earlier.

"Where?" I asked him, grabbing him by the shoulders, which caved in as I gripped harder. "Buster, Buster Fenton, where did you see him?"

"Don't wanna talk about him, that supercilious . . . ." he couldn't finish. "Wanna talk about you. Stealing home. On Satchel Paige. Sublime, heavenly, celestial." He closed his eyes and smiled dreamily to himself. Then he stared and offered to buy us a drink.

"But where did you see Buster?" Herman shouted.

"Yeah, where?" I shouted too.

"Around," he gestured lazily. "Around."

"Around where?" shouted Herman.

"Not here," he said. "Never here. Snoot."

He sat down on a wooden stair in front of a house with a porch. He told us that it didn't matter where that college kid was now. He was gone. "Gone," he waved a hand. "But he's not stealing home, no, sir." He wanted to buy us a drink, though, since he was happy to have met us. "But there's no money left," he patted his trousers. "Not a nickel left." Then he slumped back asleep, and no amount of jostling could wake him. (I'll add here that the next time we played in KC, I went to "The Afro-American" office to read David Lincoln Jones's sports by-line for this week; but there was none; and I knew then that my base-running marvel was drowned in a deep place in Mr. David Jones's knocker--pardon the play on words!)

Near dead ourselves, Herman and I picked our way back to the boarding house. As we entered the door, I thought to ask Herman if he knew Buster's real name. Glove insisted that that was his real name, though that was hard to believe. But then the subject took another turn. Since Mrs. Hamm was awake when we returned, we told her what our problem was, and she told us that Buster'd gotten a long distance call late that afternoon when he'd come back briefly from the ballpark. And before he'd had that beer with me in the saloon. Is that why his duffle bag seemed so full? I thought he'd brought it from the locker room like the rest of us. Had he already packed his clothes? Had he been killing time before the train for Chicago or New York . . . or Philadelphia?

Next day we played the Monarchs and lost badly; then we packed up and took the train to St. Louis. There was no Buster. He'd disappeared, leaving no message. We played our way back to Jersey City without him, losing eight games while winning only two. And that was that.

Franklin Byrd, who'd been so pranksome and jolly in the saloon that night, was now saggy-eyed bluer than ever; but we never ragged him, even though he lost track of his signals once along the first base line. We were down ourselves. Here we were about to go to the Negro World Series. And then we weren't. Some speculated that Buster'd been offered money by the KC Monarchs or the Newark Elite Giants and, given his ambition, had deserted us for either of them. Others opined that he'd never been fit for the Negro game, being a black man with a white man's soul, a high-toned intellectual with his nose in a book every night. Only a few of us felt that Buster had somehow fallen in with evil companions or been led astray by false inducements. I too sensed, among other speculations, that he'd been the victim of a proposition gone bad, either from a slinky, boa constrictor sort of dame or some weasel, white or black, looking to take his money.

Of course I also wondered: Could he have gone off and gotten married, having missed the girl back home? Could David Lincoln Jones have gotten it wrong in his wobbly drunkenness, that Buster wasn't stealing home?

But, no, I didn't stay long with that conjecture. If he'd gone to Philadelphia to marry his fiancée, this Jamesetta Kelly, why would he have left that glass rose in that white box with me? No; Mr. Jones was right: Buster wasn't exactly stealing home.

On this subject, I felt, moreover, that when Buster spoke of his Philadelphia fiancée he spoke too well, too carefully. She was this, and she was that: too perfect. And as he spoke, he had a peculiarly clean look in his eye, as if he was nine years old and still innocent. Then afterward he'd had a mischievous smile, meant for nobody to see. I checked my impression with Herman Glove. He could've sworn that Buster had some KC chippie in the wrong part of town--the part that Herman knew pretty well--that he ran off to visit. And sadly never returned from.

On the other hand, there was that talk of his making it into the white majors. I deduced from that that Buster'd been talking seriously to someone, some baseball businessman, some big-moneyed guy. But beyond that speculation I was stumped.

As it turned out, I had seen a few things rightly, only they were blurred. There were to be complicated developments, and these will be the substance of my story. In the first of these I and all the others were caught completely off-guard.

Once back in Jersey City, our manager Toby Hughes entered the locker room before our game with the Elite Giants. He stood in the middle of the room till all eyes turned to him. He looked solemn. He had news, he announced, that would upset everyone. He paused, and then told us that Buster Fenton was dead.

Quieter than quiet, the silence descended on us like a deep darkness. Slowly we began to look at each other--Curly and Jock and Steve and Alonzo and everyone else--and then the chatter broke like a summer storm. Where? Why? How? Who? And what exactly happened to him? The noise rose, and then Alonzo began scuffling with Henry Scoppits, nobody knew why. Soon a drowsiness overcame us, grief-struck, angry, baffled, and curious. Everyone sat now, hunched over. Then suddenly the questions popped out with new force? Where was Buster's body? Who found him? Was it accidental? Was it . . . something else?

Toby explained that the body'd been found a few days ago in Brooklyn, and get this, near Ebbets Field, in a basement in Flatbush: the basement of an apartment building on Bedford Avenue! Buster Fenton had died by strangulation; the janitor had found him hanging from a steel beam in the basement. That was all he could tell us. The death had been filed as a suicide. If we wanted to, we could go to the funeral the next day in Philadelphia, where Buster's mother and father had their home.

21

CHAPTER TWO

"Sliding on Moomba"

Strangest of all, and therefore most worrisome, was the manner of his death. Nobody got lynched in New York, at least not since the Civil War, though of course that was what everyone in the locker room supposed but didn't want to utter: that Buster had been grabbed by a race-mob and hanged. But why would that happen? I needed to go slow on this one. As for the other possibility, it is a simple fact that baseball players don't, as a rule, commit suicide. Yet Buster was different-- aloof and edgy. He was a thinker, perhaps too much of one. He was undecided about himself in a way I couldn't define. Then there was that gift he'd asked me to give his girl. Could he have actually done himself in? Pretty vaguely, it was in the realm of possibility.

Yet lynching? There'd been incidents, even recently, below the Mason-Dixon Line. But in Brooklyn? I had to go slow. Disturbing as the whole idea was, I couldn't let my imagination run away with me.

I wondered if I should pay my last respects or not. I suspected that the train ride to Philly would begin a long, serious involvement for me, not always enjoyable and not always healthy. I didn't know Buster that well; nobody did, except perhaps his fiancée. And what was her involvement in this mystery? Didn't the French have a saying: "Cherchez la femme"? We Americans have one, too: "A woman is nothing but trouble": and who was I to take that trouble?

On the other hand, I'd felt close to Buster's spirit, ever since he'd given me that glass rose in a white box and ever since that night I spent wandering Kansas City in search of him. Something about Buster needed holding onto, and maybe I'd been chosen for the job. My feeling was more than hero-worship because I was fascinated by what Buster meant in a large way. He was set for big things--and then he was gone.

And by what means was he gone? Suicide, lynching, or just plain murder? Of course, there was that present I promised to give to Jamesetta Kelly, the femme in the case, as I suspected. So I went in spite of my premonition.

I remember taking Steve Sylvester to see the musical "Oklahoma." I'd been recently discharged from the army after spending two years stateside as a corporal on the Fort Riley sports staff in Kansas (right above the state of Oklahoma). Once back, I'd met this girl in Jersey City who liked Broadway shows, so I bought two tickets for a Saturday night; and then she broke the date. Steve was also recently discharged, and he was a whistler of the latest tunes; so I dragged him along, both of us black guys in uniform, into the theater to see Broadway's biggest hit. We had a few drinks before the show to make us feel less conspicuous. We sat in the balcony. And we sobered up as the show went on. Steve loved it; so did I. In fact, I didn't want the show to end, and I sat there after everyone left the theater, until Steve had to nudge me and whisper, "Hey, man, it's over." That was my fear: the emptiness of its being over. I thought I'd never hear those songs again--except as Steve would whistle them--or see that dancing. Well, that's what two years on an army base in Kansas will do for you. And that, too, was in a sense how I felt about losing Buster. And with the manner of his death, I felt even worse.

Naturally, I must admit I was curious about his fiancée--she who'd get the glass rose. I went to Philadelphia, therefore, because I had to, honoring the dead fellow's request but also egged on by a little voice inside me that said, "Go. Maybe you'll find out the truth. Maybe that girl can tell you something that'll clear up the mystery. Or maybe the mystery is none other than she herself."

Herman Glove and I took the 8:10 express from Newark Penn Station on that hot, muggy morning in the dog days of mid-August. We sat opposite each other, looking out the window, occupied with our own thoughts. Soon, though, Herman's meditation came to an end. As it did, he interrupted mine; and I was in a mood either to talk to no one or to fight with anyone.

"What's that skinny white box for?" he asked.

Taking a deep breath, I patiently told him the story of Buster's giving it to me in KC and asking me to give it to Jamesetta if anything untoward happened to him. Herman had to think about that one. Five minutes later he spoke up again, determined, I guess, to keep from being depressed himself.

"Why do you read that?" he pointed to my magazine: I'd bought a copy of "Life" with a high-toned Englishman on the cover, but I couldn't concentrate, so I kept it draped over my knee. When I didn't answer, he persisted. "I know you can read, Moomba," he said, "because I've seen you read many things: newspapers, books, magazines. What I mean is, why don't you read material that you can relate to?" His tone had that superior smugness that usually made me want to avoid him--or slug him. "What I mean is," he continued, "a Negro publication. By Negroes, For Negroes. Have you ever heard of 'Ebony'?"

I had. But what a pain in the ass he was. And, oh, yes, he had his copy of "Ebony" ready to open on his lap.

"Then why do I never see you reading it?"

I didn't believe a magazine could solve the racial question in Buster's death. But I guess I had to speak just to keep the man quiet.

"I have read it, thank you. To tell the truth, Herm," I answered, "the photos are not so interesting as the ones in 'Life,' and there are too many ads for cosmetics, mostly for conking cream." My object was to shut him up since I was in no mood for politics. While here was Herman, for all his Back-to-Africa attitudes, with the silkiest conk on the team! As I glanced back at my magazine, I saw him automatically touch the top of his head--either to reassure himself that he still had his do or unconsciously to reveal that I'd just got him.

"Maybe so," he persisted--and, oh, boy, this was going to be a long train ride; the last thing I needed to wrangle over was black-and-white politics--"but there are other points to consider."

"Like?"

"Whose side you are on: ours or theirs."

"It's always got to be sides?" I asked. "You know that this 'Life' had Robinson's picture inside in April? He's the beginning. Then more and more. Of us." It pained me to say that, what with Buster's death so new.

"Not so," said Herman, needing to argue away his own pain. "They'll let that black boy play a few years; then maybe they'll admit a few more. There'll be a trickle into the white leagues, and then it'll stop."

"Maybe so," I said, "maybe so."

"No Dodger team is going to give its big dollar contract to me."

No doubt about that. Glove was thirty-six or -seven. His legs were tired and cramped from crouching behind the plate half his life. Right now his talk was better than his game--his game was coming to an end.

"Or you, Moomba," he added.

I put the magazine on the seat beside me. That was enough of this Moomba business. He'd been doing it all season. At first I thought he slurred Moonbeam; but I soon realized that something else was afoot. It was time to call him on it; time to have him offer me respect, at least in the way of an explanation.

"Don't you think I respect you, fool? Of course I do. That's why I call you what I do: Moomba. It's a word in Swahili for a long, slippery kind of grass. You may take it as a compliment that I use a word from an African tongue. I offer that to you because I want you to know that it's your mother continent calling to you. For recognition. For acceptance. Moomba."

I lowered my head, looking up at him from under my eyelids. Swahili, my ass.

"I do assure you," he affirmed, smiling. "Moomba means a slippery sort of grass. It's my way of saying that I appreciate your base-running ability, like as how you slip down those base paths as if you were sliding on moomba."

I could sense my nostrils expanding. My anger had grown to the degree that I had to breathe deeply to keep myself from grabbing him by the collar and shaking him hard. I realized at the same time that this reaction would be pretty stupid, Herman being Herman and weirdly whimsical in his way. And why did this Moomba business get me so worked up? Partly, I guess, from having gone on so long; partly from this allusion to Africa and the whole messy racial situation: especially now as it seemed to have gotten to Buster--and Buster's death had gotten to me. Truth was, it worked on my feelings of fear and emptiness--and these, as I began to see, were feelings I'd always associated with my African roots, whatever that might mean: but basically that futility I'd felt within myself whenever a crisis arose. At bottom, was I anything but a base runner, sliding and diving to earn my place in life?

Herman's explanation had another effect: It recalled to me a dream I'd have now and then, where I'd be rounding second base and then sliding into third, but instead of stopping at the bag I'd continue to slide--slide, slide, slide, into the dugout, through the corridor, and into a dark space: I'd slide until I awoke, fearful, with sweat on my forehead. Funny, I said to myself, that's how I feel now about this Buster Fenton affair, just sliding myself out of control and into an empty space. Some day maybe into a graveyard, mine . . . though on this day Buster's. With a quick shake of my head, I snapped to again and looked Herman in the face.

"My real name is Carl," I advised him.

"Then Carl it will be."

"I'm not a cannibal in a grass skirt," I added.

"Never said you were," he laughed.

I continued to stare at him from under my eyelids.

"Your problem," he said by way of explanation, "is that you smile too easily."

"Don't say."

"Yes, I do. You also mistake if you suppose that the black African is a savage. We were civilized way before the white man. We built the pyramids five thousand years ago."

"We also invented the peanut," I said.

"We are more civilized in our souls," he continued, "by reason of our history. We are also better athletes. You think

26

it's so terrific to play in the white leagues? The fact of the matter is the league we play in the major one. The Negro League is the best league, and the proof is that we have beaten those white boys every time we played them."

Well, not every time. But he did have a point. I nodded in agreement, although I couldn't remember a time when Herman Glove ever played a game against the white boys in the Majors. Still, he did have a point. I nodded and offered him a cigarette, which he refused. I knew he didn't smoke, but I wanted to show him I could accept what he said, even though I thought a lot of it merely self-justifying blather. I also wanted to show him that he couldn't insult me about my smile. My smile was my secret weapon, and that was something he hadn't figured out.

After this conversation Glove grew quiet, eyes turned into himself, thinking. He didn't speak for the remainder of the ride. As he seemed to have lost any sense of me, his silence got me thinking and feeling guilty: I paged through my magazine without concentration. What might I have done to keep the boy in the saloon that night--and alive? Herman, I felt, brooded about the same guilty thing as he read his "Ebony": How did the boy escape his attention? For the rest of the trip the two of us were too pensive for words.

We arrived in Philly at 9:20. Then we caught a bus to the edge of Philadelphia's West Side.

The cemetery was a small four-acre plot railed in by a black iron fence. It was disappointing. There were brown patches all over. The gray headstones, some with red and yellow flowers, looked poorly in their haphazard rows, surrounded by raggedy grass and splotches of dirt. About twenty people stood in a here-and-there arrangement around the gravesite: all respectable, the men wearing black neckties, the women behind black veils. Quietly, Herman and I extended our condolences to Mr. and Mrs. Fenton. They, in turn, nodded their sad heads and said that they were glad to meet the fellows from the Bluebirds, especially Herman, who their son had written about, praising his friendship. Then as Herman,

27

flattered to the gills, expressed a lengthy admiration for Buster, I surveyed the faces in the gathering.

I fixed my eyes on a tall young lady standing fifteen feet beyond the Fentons: She gently pushed her veil back over her little black hat, her hand moving like a bird's wing. Delicate: which was about the best I could say at the moment. Frankly, she was another disappointment. I'd expected a glamorous dish as a fiancée for Buster Fenton. This girl was plain, I thought, though neatly dressed; dressed, I should say, to perfection in mourning black, and standing there stiffly but gracefully, holding a little black purse with two hands before her. On the dainty side, she was not only tall but slender, with bronze skin, high cheekbones, a long jawline, and an indifferent nose, straight mostly until it turned up at the tip. She wore no lipstick. Below her cheekbones I detected little dimples on either side of those natural lips. Her name, I soon discovered, was indeed Jamesetta Kelly, and I saw in her the reason Buster had selected a glass rose as a tribute to their love.

But here was an ill-at-ease and sombre gathering. The mourners had no grouping at all, standing at odd spots either near or away from the coffin--silent, sad-eyed, and still. There was no opening in the ground, as the grave had not been dug. In the morning's heat the casket seemed to hover above the earth unnaturally, with no place to go. I can't say why this made me uncomfortable, but it did. Perhaps I'd visualized Buster's tombstone as large and important-looking and the crowd in mourning as upright, military almost, and filling the cemetery. Nothing seemed as it should have. Now, in this awkwardness, the minister, sweating with a white silk shawl over his black jacket, read from the Bible, then gave a little sermon, something about Buster's race being run. I admit I should have been more intent on the minister's little talk; but my curiosity was stimulated by Jamesetta Kelly. She stood alone, erect, like a statue, her eyes fixed on nothing in particular, perhaps all the more stiff in her posture when she felt me staring at her.

After the sermon there was a moment of general embarrassment. What should we do, leave, walk away, and let the casket sit there in this paltry graveyard in the hot, humid air? Then Mr. Fenton spoke, thanking us all for coming and telling us that we could go back to our daily lives. There'd be no funeral luncheon. Mr. Fenton, a mechanic on the trolley cars, had to work that day. He and Mrs. Fenton, it seemed, were naturally still troubled by their son's death, too confused to entertain company. After their initial conversation with us, after introducing us to those around, they'd remained silent: They were in deep grief. I noted, though, that Mrs. Fenton invited Miss Kelly over for an evening later in the week. And so, after a shaking of hands and a couple of hugs for the Fentons, the various friends and relations went their separate ways.

It's true, you can feel chilly on a hot day. Once we'd all gone out of the cemetery gate, I glanced back to see the mahogany coffin with its brass handles, sitting in solitude among the gray headstones, waiting, it seemed, for eternity. I felt a tear coming on, but I inhaled deeply and overcame myself. Still, I understood, Buster was truly alone now, without family or fiancée, enemies or friends. That's when the chill went through me. This was all there was.

I looked quickly for Miss Kelly. She was in no hurry, walking slowly on the sidewalk along the iron fence. By the way she sauntered, long-legged and straight in posture, one foot in front of the other, she gave the impression that she was free for the day. I felt a slight chill again, but this was my own shyness at work, since I wondered how I could invite her to lunch and then present her with the glass rose. She was not my type, you can understand, this ordinary, respectable young lady of twenty or so, because I'd only been familiar with the fuller-bodied and opposite sort. I wondered how she'd take me. I feared that she'd be aloof, as Buster often was, or even frightened, I being merely an athlete with rough edges. But it was now or never; so I slipped past the Fentons, expressing my condolences again while jogging ahead of Glove, who stopped to talk to them, and I caught up to the girl.

She'd turned to wave again to her never-to-be in-laws; they waved back sadly; and then they walked slowly away, Mr.

with his arm around Mrs.--their one child, Buster, now only a dream and swallowed up in time.

Well, my heart pounded in confusion, though this made no sense since I didn't find Miss Kelly particularly attractive. I blurted out that I had something for her from Buster. I stared for a moment, losing that sense of gloom I'd brought with me. I guess I'd gotten curious. Then I remembered Glove: Should I bring him along or lose him? I decided to lose him. So I asked the girl to wait while I jogged back to Glove, trying to figure a way to depart and still get him to meet me back at the 30th Street Station. Inspiration struck. I knew he had a passion for fancy cars. He could spend hours gazing at them in a showroom or at a special exhibit. So I told him about an item I'd noticed in "Life" magazine on the ride down, that Mussolini's Mercedes Benz, a gift from Adolf Hitler, would be on display in the Royal Hotel in downtown Philadelphia for an entire week before traveling west. If he wanted to catch it, I advised, he'd better do so now; and since I wasn't interested in anything about Mussolini, I told him I'd meet him later at the train station at three p. m. He glanced ahead to the tall, slender girl, since he understood that there was where my interest lay. Glove couldn't have been much more interested in the young lady than I. So he laughed knowingly and waved a hand, as if to say that I'd be wasting my time. But he agreed to go downtown alone and leave me to my fate with Jamesetta Kelly.

I walked briskly back to Buster's fiancée, introduced myself clearly with a pleasant smile, and explained my purpose again in speaking to her. Oddly, now that I'd started I spoke easily, without hesitation. I don't ever remember being so swift in conversation, not with a girl of her rigid bearing, though by the turn of her head she let me know that she'd be a good listener.

"I knew Buster," I began, "and I admired him. He would've been a great ballplayer. He would've been a hero in the Major Leagues. He asked me to give you this present." I offered her the box.

She stared at me (she had light brown eyes), then at the box. Without expression she took the gift; she breathed and then thanked me. Then she walked away slowly with her head down. After a few steps, she stopped and looked back at me. Had I said something wrong? Or had she done something wrong--to him? Perhaps they'd broken up before he died. Perhaps she'd betrayed him to his enemies. Why didn't she open the box and look into it? She stared, then turned away but didn't move. She spoke without facing me.

"I understand you're a ballplayer," she said. "Are you famous for anything?"

"For one thing only," I said. "Where to eat a good lunch in all the big cities of the East. Except for Philadelphia," I added quickly, hoping she might catch the hint. "Perhaps you could add to my knowledge."

"I don't know much," she replied, whirling and meeting my eyes, "but I do know the Blue Lion Luncheonette."

"I need someone to talk to," I said. "How about you?"

She nodded. I invited her to show me the way to the Blue Lion Luncheonette. We walked together for five minutes without speaking. The place was modest but cool and comfortable. Two wide ceiling fans spun under a bronze-colored, pressed-tin ceiling. Beyond the long marble counter, we found a booth and ordered iced tea and sandwiches--hers was egg salad; mine, roast beef: hers on white, mine on rye.

We waited quietly.

"You've played baseball for how many years?"

I told her seven, including the army.

The food came. We were quiet again as we started to eat.

I considered how to introduce the big questions: Why did Buster die and how? And, secondly, how might she be involved?

"Buster was different," I said.

"Yes," she agreed, nodding and looking aside.

More silence. More avoiding of eye contact. Then, as if on a strange impulse, she looked up and finally spoke: The words came as if finally released, as if she'd been holding them in her mouth and they burst forth of their own accord.

31

"He had a chance to sign with two teams," she said. "But he couldn't make up his mind."

I swallowed hard. That was a shock. I swallowed again, asking her which two.

"Oh," she said casually, "one of them was the New York Giants."

"And the other?"

"The Kansas City Monarchs."

I expressed amazement. I suddenly realized that this fiancée knew more than I thought I'd learn that day.

She went on: "That is why he came to New York. Mr. Horace Stoneham, the President of the New York Giants, paid his way."

I marveled again. Then I remembered what Mabel Hamm had told us about Buster's getting a long-distance phone call after the game in Kansas City: There it was: Horace Stoneham calling from New York.

"Buster felt guilty about leaving his team in the lurch," she said. "But what else could he do? It was a wonderful opportunity, don't you agree?"

I did.

"While he negotiated terms with Mr. Stoneham," Jamesetta went on, glancing off as if to remember, "in came Mr. Tom Baird of the Kansas City Monarchs."

"To New York?"

"Yes," she replied.

"Following Buster?"

She shrugged: "I guess."

"Did Buster actually consider signing with the Monarchs?" I asked.

"Yes," she said abruptly, then looked down at her sandwich and said nothing else.

Questions began to bubble up in my brain, and at first I couldn't say anything: Here was an authority on the case--as why shouldn't she be? So, to continue, I asked her why Buster would hesitate to sign with the Giants and instead entertain offers from a team in the Negro League. After all, we, that is, the Bluebirds were in the Negro League--and Buster had left us, as she said, in the lurch, though obviously for bigger money.

"I don't understand, either," she shook her head, looking at the other half of her egg salad on white. "I'm not much of a baseball fan," she went on. "But I know the deal with the Monarchs meant a lot more income. Maybe you might tell me about barnstorming? That is all Buster and Mr. Baird talked about: barnstorming here and barnstorming there. Buster lost patience trying to explain . . . . Because I told him that barnstorming, to my mind, seemed kind of reckless."

I had to chuckle. Right there I crossed her off my list of suspects. Reckless? Barnstorming? I went on to outline the barnstorming season, which took place after the regular season in warm places like Arizona and California.

"The best of the black players get to travel around with the best of the white players, stars like Bob Feller and Stan Musial, and they take on local teams, who always lose. But the fans out West get to see great players, and everyone has a good time. The promoters make sure the players make plenty of extra money, equal to their regular salary. Satchel Paige"--she hadn't heard of Satchel Paige until the previous week--"does it every year. It's perfectly safe."

Miss Kelly nodded. She'd begun to put things together in her head. Buster'd told her about Mr. Baird's inviting him to barnstorm with Satchel Paige and other stars, white and black, that autumn in California. Apparently, that would mean three or four thousand dollars for three months' work. Added to that would be a five-thousand-dollar contract to play for the Monarchs in 1947 season; then, of course, more barnstorming in the fall. So now Buster was conflicted. This offer was more lucrative than the one made by Horace Stoneham and the Giants.

"But the Major Leagues were the highest you could go: Isn't that right?" she needed to have this affirmed. "At a certain point the money doesn't matter. And those white players who go barnstorming, they're from the Major Leagues."

I nodded.

33

"Exactly," she said. "So Buster could've signed with the Giants and then gone barnstorming with the white players. Isn't that so?"

I nodded again. "However," I added, "it's Tom Baird who runs the operation out West."

"Oh," she said. Then she looked off, thoughtful. Now I got the impression there was something she wasn't going to tell me. But I'd only just met her: What did I expect? For all her plainness, she was a proud thing; so I kept quiet and listened when she looked back at me and continued.

The girl wanted her boy in the Major Leagues. Moreover, if Buster played in Kansas City, when would she see him? On the other hand, if he played for the Giants, he'd be here in the East, most of the time, with her. She couldn't understand his stubbornness. The more she favored the Giants, the more he praised the Monarchs. They argued. They went pro's and con's in the taxi that night--that night five nights ago when they dined with Tom Baird on 110th Street--as he took her back to her aunt's apartment on 129th Street in Harlem. Since she was a good girl, she stayed with her aunt, and not with Buster, while seeing him in New York City last week. Then Buster left her at the door and went off to think by himself. That was the last time she saw him alive.

Had she felt guilty about arguing with him? On the night he died? Did she feel she'd provoked his suicide, if such there was? That was a possibility. Her look seemed to suggest an inward conflict, a kind of self-bewilderment, asking questions that no one could answer.

"Well, then, could you explain to me," she pleaded, opening her eyes and leaning towards me, "how bad the problem would be?" She meant for a black ballplayer entering the white Majors. Evidently, Buster'd alluded to white fans harassing him for his race in Major League ballparks: that is, if he signed with the New York Giants.

"Well," I began, "it could get pretty nasty. He could get called a lot of names. He could get death-threats from the KKK types. It's a real good question. But, look, here's Jackie

Robinson ready to open the door. Let's see how he makes out. He's there to make the white game a little blacker."

"And there's Tom Baird," she said, "who makes the black one a little whiter."

As she seemed oddly sarcastic, I interjected a question about Tom Baird and 110th Street: I'd almost choked on my roast beef sandwich when I heard her mention it. Buster was out at midnight in Harlem or thereabouts with an owner of the Monarchs? And then he died?

"Yes," she affirmed, "we had dinner that night, at Helen's, a famous place: All sorts of people go there."

I said I knew that.

"Don't misunderstand," she added hastily. "Mr. Baird was full of praise for Buster. I don't blame him."

For causing Buster's death? What did she mean? I put down my sandwich.

"He stated," she went on, "that Buster impressed him as a better player than Jackie Robinson." She took a bite of her egg salad sandwich, holding it with two hands and two pinkies up. Then she placed the half-sandwich carefully back on the dish and sipped her iced tea, pinkie up. Just too dainty. Then she added proudly: "Buster was capable of excelling in many ways. He was more than a baseball player."

I supposed he was. But I didn't want to hear this. Sometimes praise of the dead sounds too formal, as Jamesetta's did now. Besides, what did it say about anything pertinent to the case?

"All together, then, there were you and Buster and Tom Baird, the owner of the KC Monarchs . . . and who else?" I asked, leaning forward over the table.

"A big fellow was there . . . with dark skin," she said; "I believe his name was Hank Thompson."

"What in the world . . . !" Thompson played second base for the Monarchs.

"A contract," she answered, reading my mind. "Mr. Baird wanted Buster to sign then and there."

"With the Monarchs?"

35

"I believe so. I supposed this Hank Thompson was there as a kind of show player--I mean, someone to show off as a prize athlete--to encourage Buster to sign."

"Did he?"

"Did he sign?" she clarified. "No. He asked to have a day to think it over."

"A day?"

"Twenty-four hours. I insisted."

"You?"

"Yes. Why? Didn't I have a right? Well, that's when Buster and I began to argue, and that's when he decided to take me home."

She didn't have any idea what might have happened after he left her at her aunt's. Did he return to the restaurant? Did he sign the contract anyway? She didn't think so. She began to get teary-eyed and then sobbed quietly. When she turned her face up at me, she seemed embarrassed. Her sadness, I said to myself, did nothing for her looks.

On another note, this Tom Baird thing began to trouble me. I'd seen him in the stands that day sitting with a friend when I stole home plate. He sat a few rows back behind our dugout. I'd smiled at him, but he registered no emotion. In fact, the man himself troubled me: I suddenly imagined him as a white killer hiding behind his respectability as a businessman in a black world. My sense of him had no real basis: but, truth be told, the man scared me. I can't say why. Of course, he should've been sitting behind his own team's dugout. But I suppose he wanted to get a better look at Buster.

Now, here was Jamesetta, Buster's fiancée, and why was she so uncomfortable with the idea of the Monarchs and the Negro League? Did her intuition whisper something strange? Or was she just being difficult and fussy? After all, what could she know about anything in baseball, white or black, except maybe the snob-appeal of the Major Leagues? On the other hand, what had Baird done to turn Buster's head? What was going on there? Hadn't Buster spoken to me, only a week ago, about a desire to be the number two Negro ballplayer in the big leagues? Then what was this footsy-tootsy with the Monarchs and barnstorming with Satchel Paige? Was Tom Baird luring Buster into a scheme to get him killed?

Best not to reveal my thoughts to Miss Kelly. Best to sound soothing.

In an effort to reconcile her to Buster's behavior, I decided to explain to her that her fiancé probably figured on doing both: that is, playing for the New York Giants and then getting a post-season slot on the barnstorming team in California, Tom Baird's enterprise. I had no doubt about Buster's powers of scheming and negotiation, trying to get the best deal for himself. She perhaps had overreacted in the restaurant. And after taking her home, Buster'd probably gone back and gotten himself an interesting proposition. And then . . . disappeared?

Had Baird gone to New York with a gang of henchmen? Was he the leader of Buster's lynch mob? But, then, what was Hank Thompson doing with them? And what lynch mob in Brooklyn? On the other hand, why would Buster negotiate so hard with Baird and then go and hang himself? Troublesome, troublesome.

At this moment I pointed at the white rectangular box on her side of the table. She looked down at it. I told her what Buster had told me--that he wanted her to have it if . . . something happened to him. She didn't react. I wondered if Buster had been contemplating doing himself in . . . or if he knew he'd run into trouble . . . and with whom.

"Please," I said, "open it and take a look."

Placidly she opened the box and gazed at the glass rose.

"Buster and I had met only four months ago. We . . . well, we liked each other immediately. We decided to get engaged when the Bluebirds hired him. We were going to be married when I graduated from college," she said. "The wedding would've been next June or July." She sighed. She looked again at the red and green glass thing. As she did, she spoke of herself.

She was going to be a teacher. He too . . . if . . . other things hadn't happened, that is, if he hadn't so much talent as an athlete.

Interesting little twist there, I thought: I tried to see the kid as a college professor--with horn-rimmed glasses, a goatee and mustache, and a tweed jacket. No, not him, not with his wide shoulders and determined jawline.

"He would've been great whatever he chose," she said suddenly, defiantly.

I nodded in agreement, even though I believed that he was meant for baseball and only that. But from her I'd got the impression then that reminded me of the impression I had of Buster, how he spoke of his fiancée as an ideal. She seemed to see him in that light also. Is that what makes a great romance, I wondered, where the two parties see each other as images of perfection? I had not known that sensation.

I'd been married for a few years to someone I don't care to name; she was a beauty, and a dandy on the bed sheets, but nothing for the long run. I'd been in the service, and when I received my discharge she was gone. In my absence she needed to be dandy on a lot of other bed sheets. So I swore to myself that I'd live a simple life, swinging a bat and running bases, reading some books and magazines and then going out drinking with the boys. But then this Buster came along, a little larger than life, certainly different from the other guys; and now he was dead. What I feared in attending his funeral was exactly this, an involvement that gradually would take me out of the small world I lived in and bring me into another sphere, grander but chaotic. And now, as I spoke of Buster to his fiancée, I felt she began to have a hold on me, her seriousness, I mean, and her plainness: as if I found her pathetic and needing my help--for Buster's sake.

And she? Was she a daughter of some publisher or doctor or lawyer or minister in the African-American community? Some refined and respectable miss, the black socialite Miss Kelly of Philadelphia's North Side? Opposed, I say now, to the white Miss Kelly who was to become the Princess of Monaco? For sure, no African prince was going to come and sweep this Miss Kelly off her genteel feet. Yet she did have class: yes, that's what it was, class: that's what captured Buster's interest in her. I felt a bit plain myself, sitting across from her in the Blue Lion Luncheonette; so I was glad to hear that her daddy was a bus driver, because I didn't want her to think that she could require things of me.

And yet . . . what else was it about her? A certain proud sadness in the loss of her hero? A confusion as to what to do next? Here I was, out of loyalty to Buster and out of sympathy for her, ready to offer her serious consolation: something also to keep myself from getting too depressed.

Uncharacteristically, I began to talk non-stop--about the racial situation in general. I guess I wanted to sound like an authority too.

We had to consider history, I said--the big picture. Now that the war was over we were ready for real change. Some folks might be hurt in the process, but black folks could no longer be ignored. We'd fought the war along with everyone else. We were part of the victory. Now one of ours, Jackie Robinson, would soon be playing for the Brooklyn Dodgers and taking them to the National League Pennant. We'd win in the Majors too. Then we'd get our rightful recognition. There'd be trouble along the way, sure, but it would happen.

Not quickly and not easily. The newspapers were discussing the inevitable step, the Robinson story. It was big. But, and here I looked deeply into Miss Kelly's curious brown eyes, not everyone was overjoyed about having black players in the Major Leagues. There were the sons of the KKK in the South and the Midwest; and situated opposite them, in a racial sense, were the owners of the Negro League teams--who ironically were on the same side on this issue. One of these owners was this Tom Baird, who'd made a lot of money with the KC Monarchs. He was a businessman, a sort of octopus with tentacles reaching out in all directions. He worked with big money players like Satchel Paige, racketeers like Gus Greenlee, and others like himself, businessmen out to make a buck. He stood to lose a fortune if the likes of Buster Fenton deserted for the white majors, and he would not go down, I believed, without a fight.

"So you know a lot about this difficult situation," she commented.

"I didn't know I did until now," I replied, a bit surprised myself at what I had inside me.

She smiled, pleased though not happy.

Well, now I'd puffed myself up so much with this talk about the leagues that I felt confident enough to pursue another possibility.

"Have you ever seen a professional Negro team in action?" I asked her. "I know you must've seen Buster play in some local minor league game, but I don't remember noticing you at any of our games in Jersey City."

She shook her head. "I've been working."

I looked her up and down. Some worker.

"As a chambermaid," she added. "In a nice hotel downtown."

"Ah," I said.

"And so many of your games are on the road."

Indeed they were.

"I'd hoped to see the Bluebirds play in the Championship Series," she said.

"We have seven home games through this week and next," I began. "Maybe you could visit with your aunt in Harlem and come over to Jersey City . . . . Actually," I spoke as a thought had struck me, "I could come by and pick you up. At your aunt's? This coming Sunday? After church?"

"Are you a single man?" she asked, cocking an eyebrow, as if there might be a doubt.

I told her my situation. I'd been married until my wife got sick: sick of my being in the army. Maybe she'd been sick before that, what with my being on the road and traveling around with a team known for its wild fun and frolics. But she'd had her own need for fun and frolics. It was no real marriage. Since then I'd modified my ways. I'd become responsible, and I knew how to treat a lady as a gentleman should.

"Buster always showed his respect for me," she said.

I believed that. I'd judged immediately that she was not easy.

"Then you will find me at 12:15," she said, "in front of the Abyssinian Baptist Church, where the Reverend Adam Clayton Powell, Jr. preaches. On 138th Street off Lenox Avenue."

I replied that I knew exactly where to find her. I shook her hand across the table. It was a date.

"Could I take you home, Miss Kelly?" I offered.

"I would like to sit here alone for a while," she answered. Over her glass rose and her iced tea.

"I understand," I said. But I did have another question. "Was that his real name? Buster? Surely, that wasn't his Christian name."

"I don't know," she confessed, puzzled. "I never supposed it wasn't. That was the name his parents called him." The minister too. Dead end, there.

I paid the bill and left to meet Herman Glove at the train station.

With that the reaction set in: fear and emptiness. Buster was dead. I'd left him in a casket all alone in a little graveyard. And now I was going to take his fiancée to a ball game. What was I stepping into? The Buster Fenton Case? No, no. I was not one to go poking my nose in other people's business. I was a traveler; I preferred to leave the past behind and travel on to the next point in time--or the next ballpark--or the next base on the diamond! What I liked about Negro proball was exactly what Miss Kelly didn't: playing a few games in one city, then win or lose leaving that town and going to the next. Come autumn and winter there was Mexico or Cuba with tours and pick-up games in areas of low expenses and high respect for you as a ballplayer and a person of color. In the spring it was back to the states with bigger money, meaty hamburgers, and smooth green felt pool tables; and if you didn't get too much respect in one town there was always another spot to hit the following day.

I had one major disappointment in my life, and that had nothing to do with my ex-wife or spending the war years in Kansas. It was my failure at the 1936 Olympic tryouts. I'd heard about Jesse Owens; I'd seen his times; and I was sure I could beat him in the hundred meter dash. I was twenty-one years old, nearly the same age as Buster, and all-too-conceited. Nobody'd touched my heels at Morgan State, not in the hundred or two hundred. Who was this Owens, anyway? So I celebrated my victory the night before by drinking a few quarts of beer and waking up the next day with a huge headache. My stomach was none too good, either. I tried some aspirin, but no luck; I was bummed out. At the track I ran four heats, coming in fourth every time. I didn't qualify for the team, and I still remember that wiry Owens crouching and clawing the grit, then leaping forward and seconds later hitting the tape. I hated him; yet I also admired him. He wasn't afraid to win. In the outcome he got his medals, and I got a little wisdom for my foolishness.

So now this death of Buster Fenton's troubled me, threatening my shell of complacency. Fear had me cast an imaginary glance at Boondocks Cooney with the cotton in his head instead of brains. I wondered if I wouldn't be better off like him, because now I began to ruminate about my place in life: about how involvement with Jamesetta Kelly would ask more of me than I could muster; about how thinking too much about Buster's disappearance and death would challenge my sanity; about how believing I could tackle this issue might get me killed just like him.

But that girl: Why had I been so quick to attach myself to her? Immediately I regretted setting up a date with her. Yet aside from her--and I prided myself on my ability to walk or run or slip away from any woman--there was the intrigue of the death itself: by hanging, in an apartment house basement, right by Ebbets Field, home of the Brooklyn Dodgers, the team that signed Jackie Robinson! What might be the connection? Beyond that strangeness was the boy himself, that handsome, aloof, powerful, sock-the-cover-off-the-ball Fenton, twenty-two years old (as I'd heard from his mother), who'd never shine like the sun he might've been in the Major Leagues--and whose accomplishments would go unrewarded and overlooked for his short moment in the Negro League; would fade into that dark obscurity of Negro potential and die in nowhere: as would be the case with any of our black stars now that the Negro Leagues, past and present, were setting into the horizon at the end of their day.

I guess I saw that Miss Kelly was a way to hold onto Buster.

I chewed on this and other thoughts as I came upon Herman waiting for me at the ticket counter in the 30th Street Station.

"It's eighty-five cents," he told me, indicating the ticket in his hand. That was Herman all over. He might've saved me the trouble by buying two tickets to Newark; but he needed to be certain of my cash, as if I'd ever not shown up or put in my share!

Then I asked him, "What do you know about Tom Baird?"

"Baird? He owns the KC Monarchs, Moomba," Glove said knowingly, "uh, that is, Carl."

I said nothing but kept on looking at him.

He looked back at me. But I knew there'd be more.

"I happen to know that he talked to Buster out in KC two weeks ago. Offered the boy a contract to play for KC. Two hundred and fifty dollars a week starting in August, that meant now, this month. With a chance to go on tour with Satchel Paige in California."

"Buster tell you that?"

"He did. He asked my advice," Herman paused. "I told him to take the man's money."

"You never cease to amaze me, man," I shook my head. "You sent him in the opposite direction! Out West. I'd've thought you'd advise him to go East, to play ball for Haile Selassie in Ethiopia."

He almost smiled. For my part, I believed that Jamesetta Kelly's information was right on the money. That meant that Tom Baird was indeed a sort of wizard in all this . . . this mystery. Troublesome, troublesome.

"He wouldn't have had to worry about being lynched in Ethiopia," Glove said grimly.

I lifted my eyebrows and nodded slightly: lynching, yeah, Glove couldn't resist bringing that in.

He breathed heavily. Then with one long inhale and exhale he brought himself together.

"It wasn't Baird," Glove said. "He didn't kill Buster. He was crazy about him." He wasn't being sarcastic. He was returning to his Negro League attitude. "I'd play ball for Tom Baird. The man's not cheap. It's him and some others, like Effa Manley with her Newark Elite Giants, that'll keep black ball alive."

"That's where their loyalty is because that's where their money is," I said. I was troubled again and didn't want to carry on a conversation.

"About Buster and the New York Giants," I opened a new topic.

That started him up again. "Something else you may not know. The New York Giants contacted Buster in KC. They sent that scout out to watch him: Bill Clancy, the fat guy with the cigar in his mouth up behind our dugout."

I remembered him, too.

"'Course you do," he asserted. "Not too many fat white crackers up behind our dugout in KC. You thought he might be looking at you, stealing home plate from Satchel Paige. I saw you flash him that fancy grin."

"Never know who's watching," I said. "But I am sure that if you were catching for KC and not Jesse Rogers, you would've made the tag." I smiled my fancy grin.

He refused to acknowledge my compliment or my smile. In fact, we didn't speak until we entered Newark Penn Station. Instead, Glove pulled out his copy of "Ebony" magazine, which he spent the rest of the trip reading. Now that I'd calmed myself, I laid my reading material aside for a while and began to speculate.

Does a man get killed in the business of baseball? This was America's pastime, for young and old, rich and poor, for black as well as white. How could it prove so dangerous? True, a good part of the Negro game depended on rackets, especially gambling, and these were run by racketeers, some of whom wouldn't hesitate to cut a man's throat. But Tom Baird? And Horace Stoneham? In the rackets? Really, now. But, then for some men, as for the moon, there's another, hidden side. And you don't have to be a racketeer to execute a murder. No KKK in New York City, either. No lynching, I supposed: but maybe just plain bad business?

What might it be? Buster kept himself clean, so far as I could tell. But was he a gambler? Did he have a big mouth, going around yakking about something he saw? Was he a rambunctious troublemaker? No, to each of these. Well, then, what kind of pickle did get caught in, and and how did he get tagged out?

As I thought and thought, the train pulled in to the platform, and we de-boarded. Before separating from me, since he had friends in Newark, Herman stuck his "Ebony" magazine in my chest.

"Here," he said, "you take this one. I'll take that."

"Sure," I said laughing. We traded magazines. The cover of "Ebony" had a photo of the lovely Lena Horne, who in my opinion was a true beauty, far above Jamesetta Kelly. Honestly, I felt guilty thinking that, but what could I say? I paged through the rest of the magazine on the local into Jersey City. There were lots of ads, mostly for women and mostly about gunk for kinky hair. One model had the same hair-do as Miss Kelly, a smooth pageboy, parted on the side and falling to the base of her neck, with a curl over the forehead: and I guessed that was okay for a woman. Elsewhere appeared a pictorial of black ballplayers getting ready for the Majors. Among them were Don Newcombe, Roy Campanella, Larry Doby, and Hank Thompson. The focus, though, was on Jackie Robinson, who sat in one of the photos with the unlikely hero of black Americans, Brooklyn Dodger owner Branch Rickey, the one white face in the entire publication.

In another year, perhaps, Buster might've shown up on these pages. He had the quiet determination and the strong individualism to succeed against the odds in the white majors. No chance now, I muttered to myself, no chance now.

CHAPTER THREE

"Hollow Dog"

Next day, Wednesday, we had no game. I woke at nine. I walked around the block once; then I tried reading a book; then I listened to the radio. I was super restless. Either that or simply crazy. I left the boarding house around ten and took the Liberty Street Ferry to Manhattan with the purpose of visiting Mr. Horace Stoneham at the Polo Grounds. It made no sense for me to go; but it seemed, on the other hand, the one thing to do that day.

It all came from the talk I had with Toby when I returned from Philadelphia and found I'd missed the practice game. Toby'd played the regulars against Franklin's second-stringers and lost. Lost ten dollars, to boot, and was in no mood to hear my excuses.

Man, oh, man, the practice. I'd been so distracted by Miss Jamesetta Kelly I forgot that we were breaking in a new kid, John Ellis, as a utility infielder. But hadn't Toby assured us we could go to Buster's interment? That is, if Glove and I'd make it back in time. Well, we didn't. I got there around five, and Glove never showed. He'd forgotten, too, and gone to see his friends in Newark.

There I was in the clubhouse, slipping by the players, all towels and undershorts, cooling off in front of their lockers, after a hot day in the sun. A few gave me suspicious looks as I directed my feet to the manager's office. I moved fast, head down, avoiding any remarks or confrontations. Did I feel foolish. My only defense was that I'd never missed a game, never'd been late for one, either. It was starting, I told myself: the Fenton Case taking me down the long road. And here I'd been dragging Glove along with me.

Toby made believe he didn't know me, letting me stand by his desk for several minutes as he wrote into his log-book. What did he keep in that thing: notes, ideas, batting averages, gross at the gate, bets?

"Toby, I . . . ."

"Moonbeam who?" he said, eyes on the page. Yeah, he'd go easy on Glove for missing the practice, since Glove was a bit eccentric; but me, no.

I couldn't begin to explain before he started in with his Useless-Nigger routine. I was nigger this and nigger that for the next ten minutes. I'd heard him toss racial names at Alonzo Emmett and Curly Strong, but these boys were heavy drinkers and nobody knew when they might not show up the next day after a party. But me? I hardly deserved this treatment. To be called Carl with respect finally by Herman Glove and then nigger by Toby Hughes on the same afternoon, it was too much. I'd entered the room a golden brown and in no time I was blacker than the tar paper on Boondocks Cooney's one-room shack in rural Alabama. I started to get emotional, and Toby could see it on my face, so he slowed down. What's in a name? It can be heaven or hell or any place in between.

"And the reason we are not the Majors," Toby alluded to the sentiment that Herman had been opining more and more, that we were the Major League, "is because we get hung over because we can't keep ourselves sober! We can't get ourselves into uniform on time! 'Stead we go out and get ourselves killed . . . !"

This was an unpleasant accusation: implying that I didn't show because I was drinking last night and that he supposed I'd gotten myself killed, like Buster, out of drunken depravity. Had Toby been that worried? Even if he was, he might've shown more respect for the dead. Or did he know things that I did not, as for instance how Buster died? Or was he only angry over losing a bet, as he went on to tell me. I think that was it.

"Some practice game," he shook his head. "Franklin"--that would be Byrd, the first base coach--"played a man with one leg. He stole second base because I had to put in that kid, that John Ellis, as a replacement for you! He muffed the tag. Then the one-legged man scored on a single. Where the hell were you?"

I dithered whether I should answer honestly since that nonsense about the player with one leg was so dopey a story-- and wasn't the practice to fit Ellis into the team? But I decided to be decent, even after all Toby's racial abuse. I decided to turn the other cheek. I promised to pay the man the ten dollars he lost betting against Byrd's second-string team, if only he'd shut up and listen to me.

Toby was a big man, in a sense. He had a thick bull neck set on top of a barrel-like chest. He'd have been imposing if his legs were proportionate to his torso, but they were short: So he was about five-foot-five, more impressive sitting down than standing up. Even at forty-five years old, he was no man to tangle with, as he weighed about two hundred and twenty pounds. The boys on the team gave him no guff. A good thing, because we all needed discipline once in a while, some more than others. But he knew where I'd been that day; and for all his toughness he might've still had a heart for Buster instead of a dark space. But who was I to tell him?

At any rate, my punishment was over with that ten-dollar offer, except that I'd have to sit out the second half of tomorrow's game and give the last four innings to Ellis, whether we were winning or not. Toby made no sense. He'd make decisions based on emotion. And on whether or not he'd lost a bet. For all his bulk, he had feet of clay. He made bets on his own, and he took bets from the players, bagging for the bookies, his excuse being that he had a wife and two kids. If he lost money, he hurled nasty language at everyone and stayed in a pet for days. Today he remained stubborn. Tomorrow I could sit and watch the Bluebirds lose another game, watch my substitute Ellis boot another play: Toby would show me who was boss. As I noted, too, that his grief over Buster's death was short-lived, I wondered if his anger didn't have an extra knot, that is, if he knew more about the death than I could guess and in some way have been part of it. For money.

"You felt close to that fellow?" he asked.

Then, on the other hand, I had to talk to someone I could rely on for information, someone a little more out there than I was. So Toby was the man. I had to chance that he was not implicated in the crime, if crime there was. I was sure I could catch him if he waffled in his answers.

"About Buster," I began.

"What about him?" he returned to making notations in his book.

"What do you think?"

"Nothing. He's dead."

"I mean," I persisted, "the manner of his death. I know you were unhappy about his leaving the team in KC, but even so, didn't you just suggest that his death was other than suicidal?"

Toby laid down his pen.

"You change your name to Dick Tracy?" he asked. "You entering the field of detective work now that you are fired and have no future in baseball?"

"Now, Toby," I said, "enough joking. That kid had promise. Why was he buried in a little graveyard in West Philadelphia? So soon, I mean, after he left the team? Why was his body found in Brooklyn? And the cause of his death, a hanging? How do you know it wasn't some sort of business-style lynching?" There, I'd finally said it. "You know, by some people hating the idea of a black player getting into the Majors?"

"Niggers always getting into trouble," he muttered, picking up his pen and scribbling in his notebook. "Lynching," he made a face of disgust, "you got to be kidding. This is 1946. This is New Jersey. And if it isn't New Jersey, it's New York. And you know what I mean about niggers always getting into trouble--with other niggers." That is, with sex, gambling, or drugs.

"You shut up, Toby," I said, angry. "You stop that talk. I don't like it." He looked up. I'd never spoken so directly to the man. "Where's your heart?"

"My what?" He squinted as if he'd never heard the word before.

"Heart."

He stood.

"What you want from me, boy?" Now it was his turn to look dangerous. But I held my ground.

That is, I stood there with my legs against his desk. But I also smiled; a hard yet understanding smile, notifying him that I was friendly but I would not be bullied. I spoke softly: "You can call me whatever you want, Toby. You know that. I'm just a street kid from Baltimore. And I ain't going nowhere in the big leagues. But Buster was another story. He was our Jackie Robinson. You and I know that he'd have given that fellow a run for his money. But he's gone, and nobody cares because he's just another nigger? It's bad enough the white man calls him that. Why do we? That's why I'm troubled," I concluded.

He kept his eyes fixed on mine.

"I'm troubled too," he said, sitting down.

"You are?"

"'Course I am. We were in for all the big bananas this season. Now we've got nothing. No chance in hell. We just gotta scratch by."

"Especially hard," I condoled with him, "with a wife and two kids." Was he serious? But then--

"Horace Stoneham!" he blurted out suddenly.

I repeated the name. "Of the New York Giants?"

"Of them," he affirmed. "That fat vanilla wafer, that miserable ofay, that, that owner"--as if this were a curse word--"he promised me five hundred dollars for Buster!"

To buy him?

"Right. To trade him, deliver him, buy him, whatever you want. To keep him away from Tom Baird in KC and Bill Veeck in St. Louis. To guide him in the right path. To work the deal. After the season. After our winning season in the Negro League! And then the kid takes off, lured to New York by that cracker, by money offered behind my back, without my knowledge!"

Toby glared at me. I nodded, blending with his indignation.

"Really a shame," I said. "But how did that get Buster killed?"

"Who said he was killed?"

"I thought you said . . . that is, I meant dead. But don't you suspect . . . ?"

"Nothing. I don't suspect nothing. Why should I? The kid screwed my hopes to the wall."

"Still . . . ."

"Maybe you should keep your nose clean. Maybe you should come home on time and concentrate on playing baseball."

"Maybe I should go and talk to Horace Stoneham."

Toby did a take, dropping his jaw and staring at me with a blank eye. Again, I surprised myself by saying that. I wanted nothing more than to avoid any deep involvement. I did, however, want some answers. So there it was.

"One more thing, Toby," I said. "Was Buster the boy's real name?"

He continued to stare, drop-jawed; then he resumed a normal expression and shrugged. "S'far as I know." He paused, thinking; then added, tightening his mouth on one side: "It had nothing to do with baseball. That's what I think." He nodded with certainty. That conclusion came into the room, it seemed, like a bird that fluttered down and settled on his shoulder. That's how hints of truth suddenly come upon us, but if you'd've asked me then, I'd've shook my head and laughed. The notion was too far out in left field.

I soon forgot about Toby's suggestion that Buster's death may have had nothing to do with baseball. I thought only of Stoneham's interest in Buster. I wanted to know if Buster had actually dealt with the Giants, maybe signed a contract. What was the harm in that? That was opening the book to page one, that's all. I knew the Giants were on a road trip through the Midwest that week; so I hoped to find Mr. Stoneham in his office, up around the clubhouse there, in the dark vacant depths of centerfield: I had a vivid picture of him there, with a golf club in his hand, practicing his putting technique--like I'd seen in the movies, the company presidents, when no one was around, shooting little white golf balls into overturned beer mugs.

Now here I was riding the IRT up to the Polo Grounds. I tried not to be too self-conscious; but how I got the guts to go through with this I do not know. Desperation, I guess, born of Toby Hughes' total lack of concern for the best player he ever managed. That and a deep heaviness in my heart; and maybe a real curiosity.

Once there, and not knowing where to find the office from the street, I decided to use the regular ticket entrance. I had no trouble getting into the ballpark; staff workers saw me as another maintenance man coming to work. I took the long walk across the empty field and up the black steps of the clubhouse, itself painted black. After a couple of long breaths I went in and then opened the door right into the secretary's office. Did I have an appointment? I could feel my lips get cold and a gathering thickness in my throat. I chose now to do what I was used to doing--though I disapproved of it always--whenever I felt out of my depth: deliver a smooth lie with a charming smile. So I explained that the owner of the New York Giants had called me about a contract to play baseball for the team next season. And my name? Well, here I started again. What else could use but my quick wit?

"Hank Thompson, miss."

She buzzed Mr. Stoneham on the intercom.

"A colored person to see you, Mr. Stoneham," she kind of whispered, "a Mr. Hank Thompson?"

"Send him in," came the voice through the speaker.

"It's okay," she said confidentially, nodding. "You can go in."

Not a large office; dimly lit. Not lined in mahogany either, as I'd imagined it. Just a space with tan walls, a pair of windows, and two leather armchairs facing Stoneham's desk. No rug on the floor, just brown linoleum. It was business, just business. Mr. Stoneham was not putting a golf ball into a glass mug, as I'd pictured him. On the walls were framed photos of him and his ballplayers, a few rows of shelves with books and trophies; he had a file cabinet to the right of his desk--and most noticeably, there was a large dog, a German Shepherd, standing on a low platform in front of it! At first startled, I realized that

53

the animal was stuffed; so pretty goofily, with just a glance at Mr. Stoneham, I went forward and petted it! When I slapped its hairy sides friendly-like, I understood that the dog was hollow! Stepping back then, I grinned stupidly, my worst sort of smile.

The man sat behind his desk writing, much like Toby did on Sunday. Now, Toby may have been worth a few hundred dollars, but this gentleman must've had a million! He wore a suit with a white shirt and tie. Mr. Stoneham was large-chested and chubby-cheeked, with bushy eyebrows and graying light brown hair combed straight back. He must've been forty or so and had eaten well all his life. Unlike Toby, he was a fellow who looked as if he'd strain himself if he exercised at all. I could hear him breathing as he wrote. He looked up at me twice, not letting on that he saw me pet his hollow German Shepherd. The second time he said:

"You're not Hank Thompson."

I smiled even harder. Time for another slight prevarication.

"No, sir, I said I was a friend of Hank's."

"He in trouble again?"

"No, sir, Mr. Stoneham. Leastways, I hope not."

"Then why are you here? Why'd he send you? He wasn't due in town until later this week."

I'd heard about Thompson, the young black second baseman being courted by the Giants and the St. Louis Browns. I'd seen him play, too, when we were in Kansas City. It was said that Tom Baird kept him very close and paid him well to stay with the Monarchs. Thompson had power; he was good for home runs. But he was a roughneck, so I'd heard, quick to get into a brawl over nothing. I considered myself lucky to have gotten this far with his name. Now I had to leave this Thompson ploy and get down to business. I hated jumping from one lie to another, as if I bounced on a trampoline of self-delusions. Still, I couldn't stop. I just bounced around.

"Actually, Mr. Stoneham," I confessed, "I'm Buster Fenton's cousin." I was apt to close my eyes here and brace for the reaction. But I could see that Mr. Stoneham had paused in his labor of the pen, searching for the right response. His eyes had a twinkling sadness, and he nodded slowly, letting me know he understood that a tragedy had touched my family. I knew then that he was not about to call me a liar and chase me out. He inhaled. He gazed over my head for a moment. He nodded again.

"Sit down, Mr. Fenton, if I may assume that is your name," he said.

"Jake, Jake, Jacob Fenton," I offered, extending my hand. We shook. I sidled back a few steps. "I, uh, I came here to ask about Buster's contract," I began. "I used Hank Thompson's name because I figured that'd sound more familiar to you." Which made no sense since he'd have known Buster Fenton's name just as well.

The man's head perked up, as if he'd heard something in the distance. Then he waved his hand back towards himself, signaling for me to come closer and sit in a leather chair catty-corner to the desk. Once I sat, the dog's head hung forward about two feet from mine. Its mouth was open, showing its teeth as if it were smiling. The chair was comfortable, soft, making me sit way down, so that when I looked at Mr. Stoneham I had to raise my eyes to his comfortable, portly figure. When I looked away I stared right into the German Shepherd's mouth.

"I'm sorry about what happened to your cousin," he said, looming over me at a distance of five feet. "We were interested in him, as you probably know. Some secrets don't stay secrets very long, especially in families. Buster was an impressive young man; he would've been--so we hoped--a great ballplayer. But such is a fellow's destiny. The Lord giveth, and the Lord taketh away. You understand, though, that I'm not a religious person; I'm a businessman. We had nothing as yet in writing. There was no contract. You understand," he emphasized, "we hadn't spoken of money."

"But you had spoken."

"There was no talk of money," he repeated. Then opening his desk drawer, he fished around for a few seconds. "Okay, here," he held out a five-dollar bill. "For flowers."

If there was any guilt there, that fiver would have hardly covered it. Actually, I'd found out what I came for: it wasn't the five-dollar bill. So I told him that the funeral was over, that Buster was already in the ground.

"Well, then, something for the gravestone."

I thanked him for the contribution. And that was that. But I'd confirmed that the New York Giants had been negotiating with Buster Fenton--and this was one of the reasons he'd left Kansas City that night and came to New York. I rose from the leather chair. Then I folded the five-dollar bill into my wallet, thinking it would help pay my carfare for the investigation, going back and forth into Manhattan. I nodded to the dog, patted its head, and began to shuffle back a bit, though I wasn't ready to leave. There was one more critical question I had for the man, about whether he thought there'd been a crime committed; but as I tried to form the words, I heard something more from Mr. Stoneham.

"Oh, yeah, Jake," he said. He paused, sitting and adjusting his position in the chair. "I believe I should say a word about your cousin's character." As he stared at me, he winced into his meaty cheeks and his eyes seemed to twinkle again. He seemed to smile. "You may have known about Buster's professional life. And publicly he conducted himself like a gentleman," he paused again, closing and then opening his eyes. "But I sense that you don't know much about his not-so-public adventures." He chose the last word carefully. "I think Buster was a good boy, basically. But he was stubborn. He wouldn't listen to advice. No, no, he wasn't involved in any criminal activity that I know of. Something worse, in a way. As least as far as the Giants were concerned. This is difficult, because I don't make judgments about people. But Buster, well, we couldn't sign him to a contract as long he consorted with a white woman."

"A white--!" I couldn't finish the phrase.

"As I thought," said the Giant owner. "This is news to you. Yes, a white woman," he went on. "Nothing personal with me, you know. But impossible for the team. At this time.

In the history of the sport. Bad, bad publicity." He shook his head.

I wanted to sit, but I didn't. A series of calculations went through my brain. I breathed deeply. I took one step towards the desk.

"I appreciate your confidence, Mr. Stoneham," I said as smoothly as I could. "But now, now I'll like to ask you what you thought of my cousin's death. You said you didn't think he was involved in criminal activity. But was it questionable in any other way?"

"Other than suicide?"

"Well, yes. Do you think he was murdered? Over, over this white woman?" Again I felt like closing my eyes before the coming storm. But there was Toby's slight suggestion, and now I remembered it: glaring and unavoidable--"Nothing to do with baseball."

The Giant owner leaned across his desk. His eyebrows drew together. His mouth scrunched up. He inhaled, nodding.

"Could've been," he said and then leaned back. He nodded again, thinking, "Could've been."

That was it? Could've been? And that was where his speculation ended. And his interest. He turned his eyes to the papers on his desk.

"What was her name?" I asked.

"That I can't tell you," he replied without looking up, "because I don't know. All I know is that he was seen with her. My scouts spoke with him about her. But he gave them no satisfaction. We think the woman is married; at least, that is what we've heard." He finally glanced back at me. "You can see how many problems . . . ."

What with a few black ballplayers just breaking into the white leagues and one caught doing up the town with a white woman on his arm. He didn't have to finish the sentence. It was still 1946.

"We were all disappointed," he commented, eyes on some paper.

Disappointed: hardly the word I'd use for my own reaction.

He began to nod as he wrote. I couldn't move.

"I wish you and your family well," he said.

"Thank you, sir."

"And a word of advice," he looked up. "Stay with the job you have. Don't try breaking into baseball. It seems like fun, but there's nothing to it. Maybe a home run or two. After that, nothing. A big headache, for all that."

I cleared my throat and left. His team was in last place that year. For all that.

"Bye, Mr. Thompson," sang the secretary, glancing up from her typewriter.

"Bye, miss," I muttered. I barely looked.

I staggered down to Central Park, walking those sixty blocks in a stupor. At 110th Street I flopped down on a park bench. How would I collect myself? This was not a smooth life, this detectiving. Much overwork of the heart. Still catching my breath, I wondered if I should pull away and take a back seat, my usual location up to now. Even with that thought, I began to speculate on the crime, as crime there certainly seemed to be.

First, it was true that the New York Giants considered signing Buster Fenton. The boy wasn't bragging when he claimed he'd be the next Jackie Robinson. Who knows what he might've been? If. But they wouldn't sign him just yet. Because. Because he ran around with a white woman, who was not only white but married! Yes, that was the meaning of Buster's secret smile that night in the saloon in Kansas City. Tch, tch, tch. Lord Almighty. Seems as Buster's nature had two contradictory ambitions, one leaning to fame and money and the other to forbidden love. Major League baseball money and his name in the record books and romance with an off-limits love-interest, married, no less. What was that kid doing? He was moving, all right. He was moving to the end of the rainbow. No wonder he was so silent and so smug. Yet what'd he need that white dame for, when he had Jamesetta? His glass rose. And what was she, the other, the play-around, that he couldn't pull away from her, not even if it meant signing with Horace Stoneham? Heavenly saints. Was it real, beautiful love or just big egotism? We'd never know now, would we?

There he was caught between that white woman and the Giant owner. He moved both ways at once. Some switch-hitter. Some pickle. Then there was also Jamesetta Kelly and Tom Baird. Stealing home, indeed.

The other side of the moon, I said to myself, the other side of the moon.

Now, what about Miss Jamesetta Kelly? Did she have any idea? Is this why she was so stiff at the cemetery? Did she know about this white woman? How could I ever ask?

I'd be taking her to the game on Sunday. Between then and my visit to the Polo Grounds nothing new occurred to me. Those same original thoughts hung over me like dark clouds. During the rest of the week we won one game and lost two. I brooded the whole time. Should I confide in Buster's widow-fiancée or keep cool? Should I take another step into this maze or forget the whole thing and concentrate instead on running bases? Maybe I'd forget Buster in a few months. If Toby Hughes and Horace Stoneham thought nothing of the boy's death, why shouldn't I? I mean, the incident was over, soon to be lost in the flow of things, while I still had a life to live. It'd been easy enough till now, so why complicate it?

Still, the boy had died . . . . And I kept hearing in my head that phrase "cherchez la femme," as the Frenchman says, and I started to believe he had something there. Of course, there were two femmes now, Jamesetta and the mystery woman. And I had that feeling of being on a night train from one town to the next, that I was moving through the darkness towards daylight and another world. Somebody had to unravel the puzzle: I felt that I, too, was part of that puzzle, part of that coming to daylight; and therefore there'd be no sense stopping now in the middle of the darkness.

But I wavered. Who was I? Certainly no detective. Sure, I'd been to Morgan State, but that was no qualification. Even so, I'd read plenty of detective stories on the long train rides to Chicago, St. Louis, and KC. So I knew something about strange, dangerous women, desperate men, and shadowy paths to truth. I knew that you had to see a lot of people and ask a lot of questions. I knew that guilt would eventually reveal itself. I knew, too, that a man could get himself badly injured sticking his nose in where he wasn't wanted. Yet all this was in the category of supposable knowledge. Which left me in a state of serious ponderation.

Then again, how far had I gone by now? I'd already begun asking questions.

Yet back again to page one; no, not page one, rather the introduction: I was only I, a stealer of bases, carried forward by the wings of chance and the moonbeam of my smile. I loved the excitement of the chase, even though you will say that stealing, in itself, isn't ethical and no one should brag about doing it. But, listen, stealing is okay if it's in the rule book; and that was my understanding: legitimate stealing--a flying into the wind to gain what would not be yours by any other right-- this was part of the game. Of life too, I realized. At the end of that run was your reward and maybe some cheers from the spectators. And maybe some better sense of yourself.

Of course, if I didn't have my speed, I'd be getting tagged out a lot and then hearing all about it from Toby. So as this principal applied to life, that is, taking chances outside the playing field, well, I was thirty years old and not a brainless adolescent any more. So I brooded and brooded. As a result, I had difficulty concentrating on the game that day. After all, sliding also meant the possibility of sliding on moomba and finding yourself floating in darkness.

Basically, I still had that hollow feeling after telling those fibs to Horace Stoneham. It was the same feeling I had when I told my track coach at Morgan State why I failed to get a berth on the Olympic Team. I claimed that my grandfather had died that very week and that I was so disheartened I couldn't get myself up to speed. Man, was that lame. Truth was, I had no grandfathers that I could remember, they having passed on before I was born. So that was it: as a first step I vowed now to avoid lies in the future, as much as possible.

The last thing I needed was to feel like that German Shepherd, stuffed with nothing!

CHAPTER FOUR

"Gnome in Brooklyn"

I'd been to the Abyssinian Baptist Church. Four of us draftees were on a tear in Harlem before we left for Camp Dix in New Jersey. We went to a show at the Apollo, we hit a few bars, we found a crap game, and then we latched on to some girls. Before we knew it the sky brightened and the sun rose red in the early morning sky. We hadn't slept a wink. We had about a dime between us. One of us suggested we say a prayer before departing to hostile places. We found the church cramped in the middle of the block with its great stained-glass window facing onto 138th Street and its gray rough-hewn stone distinguished from the three-story brownstones extending on either side of it. We entered for the early morning service. It was good to do; and perhaps my particular prayer was answered, for in Kansas I never had to face enemy gunfire. But I never saw those other boys again.

Today as I came up the street folks were bubbling out of the church in a crowd. The ladies wore complicated little hats with veils; a few shimmery polka dot dresses contrasted with the plainer colors; but all of them, the modest and the proud, displayed their Sunday polish. The men sported light-colored summer suits and either straw hats or floppy-brimmed fedoras; and the children were pictures of neatness--all nice and clean, easing out of the red church doors and strolling along the sidewalk. The gentlemen touched their hats to the ladies, and the ladies carried themselves stiff and dignified. I had to smile as I watched. Monday would bring another week and hardly genteel behavior.

I stood on the sidewalk opposite, scanning the crowd for Jamesetta Kelly, hoping also to catch a bit of her aunt, when I noticed the young minister shaking hands and laughing with his congregants. He had a suave thin mustache and surprisingly light skin. I thought at first he was a visiting dignitary from New England come to preach to his black brothers and sisters. But, no, I realized this was the man himself, the Rev. Adam Clayton Powell, Jr., recently elected to the United States Congress. I'd remembered his face from the newspaper and also from Herman's "Ebony" magazine: and there he was, dapper and friendly, standing on the sidewalk, the Harlem community's most distinguished citizen!

Shaking his hand was Miss Kelly, a mite prettier in her Sunday get-up than in the graveyard in West Philadelphia-- dressed in black with white polka dots, that same dainty hat and veil (though she'd stuck a tiny red paper rose into the hat), and all made up, red lipstick, rouge, and face powder: and there were her brown eyes glistening as she spoke, a lot brighter than a few days before. And here she was, leaving the great man to join me on an excursion to Jersey City to witness me steal home plate once again, so I hoped! I had to laugh at myself; for my vanity, that is, supposing that I'd be helping her with her mourning mood by looking spectacular on the ball field. Then I felt guilty, seeing how this girl had a fiancé who'd been two-timing her with a white woman, and here I was puffing myself up before her for applause. How much did she know about his behavior, I wondered again and again--and, if nothing, how much could I tell her--and when?

Miss Kelly saw me and came across the street with her aunt. She introduced us: "Aunt Monique, Mrs. Maynard, this is Moonbeam Slyder of the New Jersey Bluebirds."

"So nice, Mrs. Maynard," I shook her hand, bowing slightly. She was a mousey little lady, perhaps ten years older than I; she dressed plainly and carried a red umbrella.

"You're taking my niece to the ballpark in Jersey City?" she asked, not quite meeting my eye as she looked down toward Lenox Avenue.

"Yes, ma'am," I said. "If you'd like, you're welcome to join us."

"I'm not a sports fan," she replied, casting her eye in the opposite direction. She put her hand out palm upward. "Besides, it's sure to rain today. Too bad, too bad." She had a sweet, teeny-weeny voice and habit of repeating that phrase, I noticed afterward, when offering some serious observation.

"Let's hope not," I said, scanning the sky for clouds. I didn't have to look long, as perceivable westward toward New Jersey there was a looming darkness. "That would be a shame."

"It would be too bad, too bad," she agreed. "But we must accept what happens when it happens." She handed Jamesetta the red umbrella. "Here." The young lady accepted it solemnly with a nod.

I smiled.

"Goodbye," said Aunt Monique, turning and walking quickly away towards Lenox. "And be careful."

Then Jamesetta smiled. "An eccentric aunt," she commented, "but very nice." She studied the umbrella. "At least, most people think so," she added.

We started walking slowly towards the avenue as her aunt scurried ahead of us. Soon she disappeared from sight. We stopped at the corner for, well, maybe a taxi, I thought. Several minutes passed when down came the rain in a cloudburst--and the subway station, where we'd find cover, was three blocks away! Fortunately we had that red umbrella or the delicate Miss Kelly would've suffered a drenching. So would I, but what was a little wetness for me? I wondered if Aunt Monique might've gotten soaked, but Jamesetta set my mind at ease, insisting that her aunt walked very fast and had probably made it home by now.

We waited a while under an overhang from a garage; then we dashed towards the train station, managing to stay mostly dry except for our shoes.

But now the rain posed a serious problem for our date, since the game would no doubt be cancelled and I had no other pretext for keeping the girl company. I fretted about even being with this very proper Philadelphia girl, this fiancée of another man, a dead man; and I began to regret the invitation, wondering what in the world I had on my mind beyond showing off on the ball field. Of course, I did have something on my mind--the Buster Fenton Case! Surely, we could've spent the day colluding on something relevant; but now I troubled myself about what I knew and what I supposed she might not know: Buster's affair with the white lady! How could we talk about that? This business got complicated with my sense of confusion in Horace Stoneham's office; and, truth was, I'd gotten a kind of helpless feeling about it. Now this rain seemed to be a sign: maybe it was time to quit.

I got really silent for a moment, and then I shrugged when I mentioned the problem, about the game being cancelled. That's when Jamesetta seemed to have a lightning stroke of an idea.

"Have you ever been to Brooklyn?" she asked as we stood in the stairwell of the subway entrance.

Of course I had. What was her point?

"Perhaps you're curious," she suggested.

Curious? Curious about what?

"About Buster," she said. "To see the apartment house. Where he . . . died."

I could sense my eyes widen. Was I scared or only astonished that she should be so bold? And so morbid? You mean, I was tempted to say with exaggeration, where he was lynched? But why this lynching business? It made no sense, and I had no mind to startle her. She either understood or didn't. Meanwhile, she lowered her chin, her eyes fixed on me. I caught my breath and nodded. Okay. But, honestly, I'd felt a fear I couldn't explain--yeah, it was that sliding on moomba business but only a twinge. I might have thought of this myself, but would I have gone alone if I had? But now she had me, and how could I say no?

"I am curious, it's true," I began, "but I . . . ."

"I know. I'm afraid too," she said, "but don't you feel it's necessary, Buster's death being so sad and strange, that maybe we should satisfy ourselves in this particular? To see that very basement." She certainly seemed logical. She paused, watching me for a negative and cowardly reaction. I didn't have one. "I have the address," she went on. "Mr. Fenton showed me the police report. The building's on Bedford Avenue in Flatbush. We could be there in an hour."

65

"I suppose we could . . . ."

"It's an adventure," she suggested. "We'll look around and then leave."

What else could we do? For some reason I didn't want to take her to Aunt Monique's; and I was at a loss for another idea. "Then let's go," I said, surprised in realizing that she could've imagined the next important move. After all, it was obvious. Sure, I would've thought of it myself if I hadn't gotten myself into a funk that week. "Yeah, let's go. Right, an adventure. The pursuit of . . . of mystery and crime and tragedy." Suddenly my fear vanished: I'd be a hero; I'd be daring; I'd take her to Bedford Avenue in Flatbush. I'd be doing it all for Buster. And who knows how such an adventure would advance the case? I could do it. After all, hadn't I shown guts when I went to Horace Stoneham's office and questioned him about Buster? "I agree. We need to go." Just like that. I surprised myself with this rush of enthusiasm. It was to be the first of many reversals of emotion I would experience in this girl's presence during the following week. She made me feel lively, that's for sure. She too would show different sides of herself as the days went forward, some bitter and some strange. But that's to come. Right now I had that feeling of camaraderie, all the more intriguing since it was with a woman: first time for me. Even, I asked myself, if we both walked into hell? For I noted to myself that Flatbush meant mostly all white folk.

With that, I took a moment to reflect. I may have spoken too hastily when I said that the game would be cancelled. If the rain stopped, there might only be a delay for an hour at most. Now supposing I did proceed to Brooklyn, might I be able to get us to Jersey City, by cab if need be, by two p. m.? Yes, I could; of course I could. So it was settled-- off to Brooklyn via the IRT. After all, I reasoned, we dealt with a question of murder: was it or wasn't it? It would be important to check out the scene of the might-have-been crime--or, on the other hand, suicide. There could be signs pointing to one thing or another. For sure, we'd get over to Jersey in time if we had to. That was the meaning of modern transportation. That's why they had taxicabs. That's why they built the Holland Tunnel!

Wild sheets of water poured down on us as we came up out of the subway in Brooklyn. Jamesetta kept her hand over mine as I held the red umbrella. We ran, only stopping once for me to pull my sports jacket over my head; and then we continued, keeping close to the buildings until we reached our destination. All of brick, it had five stories, its entrance at the end of an open walkway lined with green hedges. In the doorway we pressed just any button, and when the buzzer sounded we pushed open the door and went in. Somebody upstairs would wait for nobody to arrive. Then, laughing, we left the open umbrella in the vestibule. After taking the elevator to the basement, we came into a tomb-like area, gray and empty except for piles of boxes here and there. It was poorly lit, dusty, and unswept; and I regretted being so quick to leave the wet umbrella upstairs. It might've done for protection, but too late now. Hesitantly, we paced around the area, trying to locate the exact spot of that horrible event.

We located nothing. But, then, what were we searching for? I began to feel creepy, the two of us alone in the cellar, a desolate place of death, so it seemed.

Then a voice broke the silence: "Can I help?"

We turned. An upside-down L of light opened into a full frame of a door against the far wall. From it, a long, fading shadow stretched onto the floor. The substance of that shadow was a small, gnomish fellow with a large head that moved back and forth. No ghost but scary all the same. Jamesetta grabbed my hand and slid behind me. I took a step backward but refused to let the figure daunt me.

"Can I help you folks?" I could hear a colored accent in that gruff voice: It said "ah" for "I" and "hep" for "help." So, with some relief, I guessed that this might be the janitor and that doorway must lead back into his rooming space.

To my surprise, Jamesetta spoke up, saying from behind my shoulder, "We thought this was the second floor." Now, that was so hollow and absurd a lie I almost laughed; I was equally astonished by her readiness to prevaricate, and in so natural a style, that I took a quick glance for a new understanding of the girl. As the basement was indeed a strange place to be caught snooping, I realized as well that awkward situations lend themselves to eccentric expressions of personality. Even so, given the situation, there was no time to psychoanalyze. I was glad she was still with me.

"The second floor storage area," I said, trying to convey some sense in her statement. "We were here to find a tricycle." Oh, yes. Always cover one lie with another. It delays anxiety. It gives you poise, momentarily. Of course, it is like sticking another foot in your mouth after you've put in the first one. I couldn't help myself. But, as I noted, we were thrashing around in the dark.

"For my niece," added Jamesetta. Were we a team?

"Ain't no second floor storage area down here," came the gravelly voice. Then all the overhead lights went on. They didn't blind us; they did, though, reveal us to the gnome: and him to us. With the light reflecting from the top of his large head, I saw that he was bald. He seemed like a shorter edition of Franklin Byrd when Byrd was baggy-eyed, tired, and cranky. Jamesetta's instinct was to panic and run, but as she bumped past me I grabbed her elbow and stepped ahead of her, shielding her from the eyes of that disturbing character some fifty feet away.

"It's all right," I whispered. "Stay still."

"Who are you?" he demanded. As he came towards us I detected a limp. He wore blue denim overalls and a blue workman's shirt. "You don't belong here," he said, stopping about twenty feet from us. "Get out." He waved his arm toward the elevator.

After making fools of ourselves with stupid lies, I debated whether it wouldn't be better now to tell the truth and ask about Buster's death; either that or turn and run up some stairway, pulling Miss Kelly behind me. But then the gnome in the blue overalls started towards us again. He came right square into us, putting his face--a smallish face under a large forehead--practically into my chest, as if he would smell me. He turned that face upward.

"Do I know you?" he asked cautiously. He studied my face.

"No, sir," I replied, smiling my nicest smile.

"You sure?"

"Yeah, pretty much."

"P'raps you came to see me 'bout somethin'?" He continued to read my face, at the same time putting forth his finger and tapping my lapel. I was about to mention our true intent in coming there; but a thought stopped me: As to his question, what might I be coming to see him about?

"Got somethin' for me?" he screwed up his mouth on one side as he rubbed his hands together.

Money? For him? Did he think I was a numbers runner?

"No, sir," I answered.

He stepped back. "This ain't no place for hootchy-kootchin'!" he shouted, moving his eyes back and forth between Jamesetta and me. "Get out!"

"We didn't come here for no hootchy-kootchin'," exclaimed my partner in this adventure. She whirled around me to confront the gnome, who stepped back a few feet. "That is no way to speak of a lady, especially in her presence!"

The janitor was struck dumb, staring at this classy lady in her Sunday polka dots. Although boldness is a good tactic when escape seems unavailable, it can expose a false position, which is exactly where we were now. Because if on this Sunday afternoon we were not in the basement for hootchy-kootchin', what were we there for? Not for Jamesetta's niece's tricycle, certainly.

I squeezed the girl's hand, hoping to communicate the idea that she should be quiet for at least another thirty seconds while I thought of another gambit. I can't say why, but there is no feeling so hollow as being caught in a lie by an old man. In a strange, dark basement. Where you don't live and where others like you don't live. We could've easily run past this janitor, as with his gimp he'd never even try to catch us. But that would've made us feel stupid and look guilty; then again, I considered, there were two of us. We were here for a purpose, and we could stand up for ourselves, at least momentarily. Moreover, I could account for my own speed but not for Miss Kelly's in her patent leather high heels. It occurred to me then to present myself as a New York City Inspector of Electricity-- or maybe his assistant--but I hesitated. Man, did I feel inept. That's when the girl popped up and said:

"I happen to be Buster Fenton's fiancée."

I closed my eyes. Jee-sus. I expected an explosion. In my mind I saw men in blue uniforms with silver badges breaking through the walls and putting us under arrest! This was a potential criminal case. It might be that the police waited precisely for characters like us to show up--felons returning to the scene of the crime! Or, if not that, witnesses to the crime. Or if not that, anyone with dark skin they could plausibly pin a rap on. Wasn't Miss Kelly one of the last to see Buster alive? Hadn't I hung out with him in Kansas City? I kept my eyes closed listening for the gnome's response.

"You don't say," he said slowly, rubbing his chin. "And who might this Buster Fenton be?"

Oh, boy. I opened my eyes. The janitor looked from Jamesetta to me and back again.

"The baseball player?" said Miss Kelly. "Who died here? By hanging?"

Now the gnome rubbed his head, then put his hand to his chin again, shaking his head. "No where to hang a rope here," he said melodiously. "Hanging? I'd think you'd have to go to Mississippi for that. Heh, heh. Certainly no hanging tree here, not in this buildin'." He was actually chuckling. "What you two colored people doin' in this neighborhood? You lookin' for a white fellow? He play for the Dodgers? Buster Fenton? Never heard of him."

Never heard of Buster Fenton?

As he spoke, my eyes scanned the ceiling for a place to loop a rope. There might've been some place. I couldn't begin now to walk around and check in every corner. From what I could see, the ceiling was pure plaster, smooth as the basement floor and almost as grimy. Quickly I turned back to the janitor.

"He was a Negro player," I said. "For the Jersey City Bluebirds." By now I'd become confused and anxious, trying to figure where in this basement to loop a rope--and how this janitor could've never heard of Buster Fenton! Surely, he was lying to us. Suddenly, I felt the urge to escape, forget about my resolution not to run. Already I realized I'd spoken too quickly. The whole game had gotten really funny, but not in a humorous way. The gnome continued to stare at me, blankly. Panic overcame me. "Thank you very much," I said. "We will be going." I guided Jamesetta past the bald-headed figure and back to the elevator.

"And who may you be?" he called after us.

"I am George Washington Carver," I answered. "And this is my wife Martha."

The elevator door opened. With much relief we rose into the light, took Aunt Monique's red umbrella from the vestibule, and hastily exited onto the sidewalk. Once outside the building, I realized how scared I'd gotten in the basement. I was again reminded of the dream-slide I spoke about when Herman Glove explained to me about moomba, the feeling that I was in the dark with no control and sliding into nothingness. Had Miss Kelly noticed my panic? That was my little worry for the moment.

"Your wife Martha?" laughed the girl. "That was too much!" She laughed almost hilariously, while I didn't think it that amusing. It was as if she'd experienced a strange release down there in that dungeon! At the time I was still breathing noisily, hoping to relieve my nervousness. I'd gotten totally disoriented!

We walked quickly towards the subway station. The rain still poured, and we got wet with rushing. Still, the rain was a good thing because it kept me focused on the real world: It was good, too, because I was in no way ready to play baseball. It was one-thirty on my watch. We might've gotten to the stadium if we had to, a little late perhaps, but that was unnecessary now that the rain kept pouring.

There were other things to think about. My mind spun. What confusion. What darkness in the basement. What turmoil. Might the janitor now be phoning the police? Or the committers of the crime, if crime there were? And if there weren't, why the lying? I had Jamesetta check the address for the building. There'd been no mistake. No, no, that gnome was party to a fake-out, an immense lie, a criminal deception! There'd been no Buster Fenton hanged in that apartment house cellar!

Scary, scary: and again that old pull told me to let it go: This was none of my business. A sense of the future whispered to me that the deeper I got into it, the darker it would get and more disorienting. Things would become difficult in the extreme. Jamesetta, however, continued to laugh. And I had to admit it was good to face the daylight, rushing through the afternoon with her, even in the rain.

"That was fun," she said as we descended to the subway platform. She held my hand as I gazed at her, the red umbrella over my head. "Now you can call me Jimmy." And I'd considered her to be so proper. One never knows. As I folded the umbrella I noticed that she looked wilder, a bit mussed up, but also natural, with an eagerness to laugh, maybe even jump up and down. Her laughter was fun to watch: she actually seemed pretty for a minute. I had the strangest image run through my mind: I wished that we were out in the country, in a wide meadow full of flowers, where we could chase each other till the sun went down, laughing and laughing. Yet I couldn't find it my heart to laugh. "Now you can call me Jimmy." She laughed again and nodded, encouraging me to say it.

"Jimmy." I had to smile. Maybe things weren't so bad. She'd set my heart beating again by her liveliness. She was no glass rose. She was a discovery. I wondered if Buster ever called her Jimmy. I started to like her for her freshness and her high spirits.

And then another strange thing went through my mind. Gazing at her, I heard the popular song "Polka Dots and Moonbeams" in my head, especially the part where

> There were questions in the eyes of other
> dancers

As we floated over the floor;
There were questions, but my heart knew
all the answers
And perhaps a few things more.

But my heart knew none of the answers, because I had no questions in my heart, so I told myself. I did have questions in my head but no answers--these would have to wait . . . until when I wasn't sure. I had to go slow, be careful. True, I began to feel light-headed and silly.

"Okay, Jimmy. You can continue to call me Carl," I laughed, because she hadn't ever called me by my real name.

She looked up at me with her soft, bright face, wet with rain. It was the moment to kiss her. I hesitated. No, no, she wasn't for me. I kind of bit my upper lip. And then a train passed on the other platform going the other way. A cloud came over that brightness of hers, suddenly, like the dark gloom that appeared in the sky over the church in Harlem. She showed that expression of grief again, the one she had as I left her in the Blue Lion Luncheonette over her iced tea. She turned away, saying, "The trains run so slow on Sundays."

Yes, the moment had passed. Actually, I felt relieved. And I began to feel saner.

What to do. We could, of course, have gone to the local precinct house. That was a thought. Just to ask some questions. My better sense reminded me that that would be the fastest way to get us both arrested, especially if the crime, if crime there was, and it certainly looked that way, had undergone a cover-up and the police needed a pair of scapegoats. Which they did, as I then recalled, because "The Amsterdam News" up in Harlem had a memory of Buster's performance on the ball field in July, and now a columnist was making a stink about about the Fenton "suicide" that he put in quotation marks. He, too, wanted to know what happened to the boy. He, too, believed an injustice was in the works. He knew who Buster was, and he wanted answers! But I didn't want that answer to be us!

We were silent as we sat on the train, going over the Manhattan Bridge and then uptown in the same mood. Why had I told her so soon that my name was Carl? Usually whenever I used my rightful name I did so to get someone to back away. I'd been Moonbeam for a good seven years, except in the army, and that was respectable enough. Till now. What, was I trying to raise myself in my own image? Or did I think that Moonbeam sounded immature or silly coming from her? I cringed a bit when she used it to introduce me to her aunt. Of course, I'd used Moonbeam also when I introduced myself at the cemetery, though she didn't use it then. She called me Mr. Slyder.

Meanwhile, I tried to work through this episode in the basement. My head smoked with speculations. I had checked and re-checked the address of the apartment house on Bedford Avenue. We'd been at the right place, but something was definitely wrong there. And after the janitor flicked on the cellar lights, I'd given a hard, quick sweep to the area: Everything was in order, no sign of recent repair work, no police markings, as you might expect--and no beam to loop a rope onto. The basement was merely dusty all over, as if no one had been there except a bald-headed gnome in blue work clothes who commonly refrained from using a broom.

"Was he doing his job or just lying?" I broke the silence as we climbed the subway steps onto 135th Street.

"Lying, of course," answered Jimmy.

I nodded and then began the questions. Why did he suppose he might know me? Why did he ask if I had anything for him, namely money? Was he waiting for a pay-off? Or had he merely won some money playing the numbers? Or further, was Buster's death so hugger-mugger that even the janitor, who lived in the basement, was in the dark? Or was he trying to keep the place respectable, not to admit to either a murder or a suicide there? Even so, how could he deny knowing Buster's name, what with this growing scandal in the Negro community? How could he not have had people, reporters, cops, and such already knocking on his door in that dusty basement? And why was he there and ready to eject us from the building on the off-hours of a Sunday afternoon? Did we need to tip him in order to stay? Ridiculous idea. And isn't Sunday the day even janitors go to baseball games?

"Very suspicious," the girl concluded.

By now the rain had stopped. I walked Jimmy, as I started to call her, down to her aunt's on 129th Street. It was strange to hear her call me Carl in return. It was like a voice from another side of the planet, a clear voice, sweet and feminine. Against expectation, I became elated when I realized it was happening. It was a voice almost spiritual. I glanced at her again. She'd been dampened and disheveled by the day's ordeal, but she seemed livelier than ever. She laughed at everything I said. Was I that funny? It was that voice, though, that brought me back to the question I had before I'd seen her at the church: How much did she know about Buster and this other woman? If she knew enough, that would explain her moods and her sudden aloofness. Below everything, it was that voice that whispered to me: "I know enough." And supposing that she might made me moody. So I was glad when she shook my hand at Aunt Monique's brownstone stoop and said:

"This has been an exciting day. Thank you for taking me to Brooklyn and down into that basement. Don't you think it was necessary? It's got me wondering, you know, because I don't believe at all that it was suicide. I hope we don't get into trouble now. I hope that you don't get into hot water with your team. Do I ever get to see them play?"

We had a date for the upcoming Saturday, when she would meet me in Jersey City to watch us against, of all teams, the Kansas City Monarchs. As I walked away I ran my eyes over the brownstone where Aunt Monique had her first-story apartment. I noticed also the other once-fashionable homes on 129th Street, considering how with a little work they'd all be handsome again. After the rain, a hint of redness glistened in the brown of the stone, which seemed usually smothered up in hard times and forgetful upkeep: How did black folks, I wondered, manage to occupy Harlem just as it descended into careworn homeliness?

But now I'd also developed a fascination for the partner of my adventure in Brooklyn.

Jamesetta. Jimmy. Jimmy. Jamesetta. I wondered which name fit her best. Jamesetta was a real pretty name; but then Jimmy had a nice ring to it. She was that proper school teacher type in her outward manner, but she was also a surprisingly spunky kid once she got going. I wondered which side I liked best. I liked both. I kept smiling, remembering how she held her egg salad sandwich with two pinkies up and how she got high-toned with that bald-headed gnome in the Flatbush basement. Above all, I realized she'd gotten me curious about how to conduct myself outside the field of baseball.

It was started raining again when I got back to Jersey City. I sat around my room, listening to the radio.

It took a while getting to sleep that night.

I may have been critical of Jimmy's propensity for the quick lie; but was I any better myself? I'd waffled and shifted from side to side in that basement in Flatbush, and then I'd taken the girl's hand and run away. I'd felt more panic than I let on. Truth was I'd lived too long without ever setting my foot down strong; instead just sliding from here to there without commitment or responsibility. And that was the problem: When things went wrong, I didn't know how to behave. I lost who I was, that is, if I ever had what I was to begin with. Sure, I could talk colorfully, always praying that my rich imagination would come to my rescue. That was no real way to get out of a fix and certainly no inroad into solving a crime.

Did I say that? Did I think I was Dick Tracy? Not by a long shot. Yet here I was, talked into going to a kind of tomb in Brooklyn, getting charmed by a girl who loved another man, and supposing that I was obligated to go forward into--into what? Sliding on moomba. Indeed I was. So, "Hold on, kid," I told myself. I had to stop and consider what I owed myself as well as Buster and of course Jamesetta, because if I proceeded I knew that I stood up against pretty hard dealing and pretty big money. How was I supposed to take purposeful action? Look at me. Here I was, gallivanting around Brooklyn and getting scared off by a gimpy, bald-headed gnome! Why? What were my reasons basically?   Had Jamesetta bewitched me? Was I idolizing Buster too much? Was I coming out of my long-term complacency?   I lay thinking for a time; then my head got cloudy as the words started getting tangled and vague; so I finally fell asleep.

I dreamed of Jamesetta Kelly running before me on an open meadow.

"Silly," I said to myself when I woke up.

CHAPTER FIVE

"Flow Motion"

Meanwhile, we won two of three games against the Indianapolis Clowns. The week passed calmly, me not knowing what to do next, just hanging around town in a kind of limbo.

As planned, Jimmy came to the game on Saturday, sitting in a box seat along the third base line. I wanted to keep her away from our dugout, where one of the guys might start talking to her and then discover she was Buster's fiancée. I wanted her to enjoy the game. Also, it was my vanity to suppose that at a critical moment she might see me streaking around second and third, heading for the plate. Unfortunately, on that day my progress around the diamond didn't carry me that far, because before long there was an incident, both painful and embarrassing. And disturbing.

We played the Monarchs with Satchel Paige on the mound. We scored no runs for three innings as the great one struck out nine batters in a row. In the top of the fourth, two out, the score 0-to-0, the KC outfielder came to bat, Leon Latortue, so-called, a new guy I didn't recognize. I remember only his dark face grimacing at me as the incident went forward. He singled off our right-hand pitcher Noah Bateson, and then on the second pitch to the next batter he broke for second. The batter didn't swing, and Herman Glove threw a perfect peg to the left side of the bag at second, which I caught to make the tag as the runner slid. As I brushed his right ankle with my glove, this Leon quickly jerked up his left foot, spikes and all, into my cheek, cutting it. The umpire called him out; and when touching my cheek to feel the wound, I heard this miserable bastard (if you'll pardon me) mutter as he leaned forward to rise:

"Next time it'll be your nose. Keep it clean."

That's when I punched him in the face and sent him down again. Within seconds both dugouts emptied, men running to second base from both sides and piling up in a slugfest. I figure thirty men were there in that melee, with the human mound growing higher and higher as the players from the Bluebirds and the Monarchs rushed in. It took fifteen minutes for the umpires to clear the field and start the bottom of the inning. With me coming to bat.

Frankly, I wished it weren't me, because I was totally discombobulated, what with my confused thoughts about the Fenton Case and Jimmy sitting in the box seats and my anger over the spiking. And there was the tall and rangy Satchel Paige on the mound, and I knew he had something interesting planned for this. He was the one person who'd avoided the fight, probably spending the time considering how he'd handle me, the Bluebird troublemaker. The crowd grew hushed as I came out of the dugout, sensing that I was a marked man. Everyone knew that Satch could hit a fifty-cent piece dangling on a string over home plate; so that beaning me would pose no difficult task for him. Advancing to the left-hander's side of the batter's box, I could feel the crowd focusing their silent attention on me, holding their breaths for a showdown between the Monarchs and the Bluebirds. Or comeuppance for the culprit who'd provoked the ruckus. All they'd seen was me punching Leon. What they didn't hear were the words Leon Latortue, so-called, spoke to me after his nasty slide: "Next time it'll be your nose. Keep it clean." I'd heard it, and that made me doubly nervous, wondering where the threat really came from and whether or not that dangly Satchel out there, all spidery arms and legs, weren't part of the conspiracy to get that nose of mine.

Before the big stand-off between him and me, Paige checked his outfield and noticed that Leon was missing from centerfield. He signaled to the dugout, and out came Leon, or was that him? He seemed like a different person; as he passed through the infield, Satchel looked twice. But I couldn't decide, I was so distracted with my own concerns. Still, this confusion bothered me. Who was this Leon Latortue? Had he been put in the game purposely to spike me? And then taken out? Was he some kind of hoodlum just put in the game to get at me? He had a mean face, as I recalled. As my head swam with speculations, I forced myself to turn and face my destiny, held in the hand of the man who'd throw the next ball towards the plate.

I brought the bat to my shoulder, choking up for easier manipulation and gripping it much too hard. I stood leaning back a bit from the plate, an awkward posture; but I needed to see the ball as it came hurtling in and then be ready to hop backwards if it came at my head. I eyeballed Satchel something fierce. Then in a friendly greeting I flashed him a ray of my moonbeam.

I thought I caught Satchel smirking ever-so-slightly back: because what happened next was not what the spectators or I anticipated.

As everyone knew, Satchel could let loose a fastball of ninety-five miles per hour. A white object would come at you looking like an aspirin tablet, and in a split second you'd have one strike against you. And so on. He could strike out whole teams, inning by inning. Now, add a touch of animosity to that aspirin tablet and understand how daunting it was to face his pitch. My tension was such that I could feel the bat shake in my hands; my thighs quivered in my uniform; and I feared that the fans could see my knees becoming unsteady. A man could die if bonked hard on the side of his head. A baseball cap afforded little cushioning against such a blow. Yet in spite of these terrors, I continued to smile friendly-like at my soon-to-be assassin. My smile was my secret defense, so I believed.

But Satchel surprised us all. As I awaited my doom, his long arms swung up, reaching high; next his left leg kicked for the sky and paused, it seemed, with his spikes higher than the button on his baseball cap. Down came the leg; over came the arm: Paige released the ball. I tensed, staring and waiting. I stared, and I waited. The longer I waited the tenser and tighter I grew. However, instead of a whizzing fastball, Paige threw a lazy never-to-arrive change-up at about forty-five miles per hour! There was the ball; it seemed to be coming across the plate. But when, when? Able, then, to wait no longer, I lunged forward and swung. The ball kept floating in even after

I swung. Finally it hit the catcher's mitt; but by then I'd pulled myself off-balance and, having missed the ball by swinging too soon, I pitched forward and fell face downward on the dirt in front of the plate.

The crowd let out a roar of laughter. The laughter continued even after I arose and brushed myself off. I assumed my stance for the second pitch, my ears burning with anger and shame.

Surely, that pitch was the slowest ever thrown in organized baseball! And I had bit. I tried to breathe normally and look seriously for the next pitch; but then I added to my shame by striking out on two more ill-timed swings on balls gently thrown by Mr. Paige. How easy it is to hate a man who makes a fool of you. Yet in spite of my frustration at that tall, gangly figure out there on the mound, I told myself to calm down and understand that I'd survived what might've been a brutal moment thanks to that same character. Even in the act of fuming at myself and him, I realized that Satchel had performed an act of grace, finessing ugliness with a touch of comedy, albeit at my expense. Secretly, I had to smile when I saw the truth of it.

Paige was an interesting fellow; I mean, beyond his skill as a thrower of baseballs.

As I was forgiving him for his stunt, I remembered that Miss Jamesetta Kelly sat in the stands right along third base (a point I never reached that day), witnessing every part of my disgrace. Even worse, I supposed that she saw the lead-up to that disgrace in my resorting to violence and punching Leon Latortue, so-called, in the face. I'd sparked all the trouble. Therefore, I made up my mind then and there: I resolved to forget the Buster Fenton Case and never see that girl again. After all, she was hardly anyone who interested me in a personal way, so I told myself. And secondly, I resolved to go see Satchel after the game and thank him for humiliating me. He'd saved my life! He released me from troubles in the future, too! So much for watching through the night in a train that would never arrive at daylight!

In the dugout I looked down the bench to see who might be gentleman enough to escort the lady to the bus stop, maybe take her down to the Liberty Street Ferry. I spotted Steve Sylvester, who knew her, since I'd introduced them before the game and asked him to keep the boys away from her. Steve was a gentleman, so I judged him to be, with a girl like her, serious and polite: the easier for her to go along with him. He agreed to accompany her to the ferry if would pay for his bus fare. I said I would.

However, there was no need for that, because as I came skulking out of the locker room, I found Jamesetta waiting for me. She'd sent Steve on his way, whistling, she said. She needed, instead, to see me. She needed to be sympathetic.

"And don't think I never would be," she scolded. "And I forgive you for trying to shake me off. I understand." I apologized.

She touched my cheek gently. "Does it hurt?" she asked. I told her the cut was a small thing. She said that I was justified in what I did. "That Leon," she offered, once I told her all the details, "deserved what he got, a bloody nose." Indeed.

She added that she felt sorry that the Bluebirds had lost the game. But she thanked me for inviting her because it turned out to be the most exciting sporting event she'd ever seen: in the which, her look implied, I was the hero.

I gave her a long, quiet look and held back my amazement. Here we had lost the game by 11-0, there'd been a brawl at second base, and I'd fallen on my face trying to wallop a forty-five-mile-an-hour floater--and all Jamesetta Kelly could comment on was my spike-scratch and my generosity in inviting her out that day! I could've kissed her, she was so sincere in her concern and her enthusiasm--and so well decked out in another Sunday outfit, a baby blue dress with a little dark blue jacket; and it was only Saturday. Well, I restrained myself.

It was no time for plunging into romance. Not with so many questions unanswered, the first on my mind being whether she knew about the white woman. And if she didn't, how long would she grieve for Buster once she did? Was she truly grieving for him now? Isn't that why she came to the Stadium today, to have a little fun and to forget? Did she see me only as a friend? Was I too humble or too slow? Was I too wishy-washy in pursuing Buster's mystery--her mystery now? It was too difficult to separate all these contingencies; moreover, I was completely intrigued. So I guess I was still in the ball game, as there was no way to leave her, not after she'd touched my cheek so tenderly and after she stood there so winsome in her two-tone blues. I sighed a bit; and then I made a decision.

"Let's go see Satchel Paige," I said, taking her by the hand. She had gumption, as I remembered. She might be of help. I figured if Satchel didn't want to confer with me he might change his mood when approached by the proper Miss Kelly. No, it wasn't to thank him for humiliating me; that impulse had passed. I had something else in mind. So why not take the bull by horns? But suddenly my gentle companion pulled away and, face to face with me, she stood stock still.

"Are you, in fact, a troublemaker?" she asked.

"Not at all. Satchel's an interesting fellow. He might be able answer a few questions," I replied.

"Such as?"

"Such as where to go next." Now, that is, our suspicions had been greatly aroused by our adventure in Flatbush.

She was unconvinced.

"Wouldn't you like to meet the greatest colored player in America?" I proposed.

She stiffened, tilting her head to one side. Her eyelids dropped.

"I thought I did, once," she said without emotion.

I turned away for a moment and drew a breath.

"That is exactly the point," I said, coming back to her. "We owe it to Buster. Now, this Satchel Paige knows a lot of people, a lot of white folk among them. He has the widest view of the game, knows the most about the baseball world and everyone in it. I think the man can help with the investigation."

"What investigation?"

"You very well know," I said. "After that business in the basement of that apartment building, can you be sure that Buster died innocently? I think not. Do we want to let the matter rest? Not after Leon Latortue, so-called, threatened me to stay away. We can be sure there's a connection. Don't we want to proceed with our inquiry? I say we do."

Her eyes widened. She nodded, and she took my hand.

In my mind, thanks to that Leon, baseball was involved as much as the white woman. So maybe Toby's suggestion was merely a half-truth.

Off we went to The Huntsman's Bar and Grille, where I expected to find Satchel enjoying a steak dinner, as was his custom, so I heard tell. I didn't know the man to speak to, except to taunt him whenever I got on base. But he knew who I was, though he never acknowledged me in a crowd. He was proud; he was also whimsical; so I supposed that if I could get past his ego he might stop and tell me a few things. When he might've hurt me with his fast ball, he threw that change-up instead: that said something about his character. It was as if he'd pulled the slipknot on all the tension and set the game back on its track. Even though he picked me as his victim, I liked his largeness: he saw the whole picture. I judged him to be a truly civilized man.

He sat in a booth inside the saloon, talking to two other Monarch players. Instead of interrupting him, imagining my appearance would start another brawl, I sent Jimmy in to draw Mr. Paige out. She took her mission seriously; I admit I behaved a bit cowardly doing this, but what choice did I have? So in she went, my cohort in the scheme to move Buster's case one step forward--into more confusion, perhaps, but still forward--bringing, if possible, some malicious intent or evidence of it into the light of day. Meanwhile I waited in an adjoining doorway.

Within five minutes she re-emerged, chatting with the tall, self-confident pitcher, showered and dressed in white shirt, tie, and sports jacket. After all, it was a Saturday afternoon, soon to be a Saturday night. When I asked her later what enticed him to delay his meal, she told me that she'd thought it best to be frank with him, by telling him the truth: that she was Buster's girl and that a black detective was on the case and had some questions for him. Most other players, at that moment, would have dashed for the back door. Not Satchel. Whether or not he believed her or only found interest in her curiously pretty face (it's true, I'd begun to see something in her), there he was. Seeing me, he backed up slightly; but since I flashed him my friendly smile, he gave a look around, then pointed his chin in the direction of a small park, where we went and sat on a bench.

Jimmy, by previous arrangement, took a stroll but kept in sight.

"I don't imagine," Satchel began, "that she is anyone's . . . now?"

"Forget the girl, man. This is serious," I said.

He gave me a funny, cocked-eyebrow look, as if to say, what could be more serious? Then he shrugged and pointed to the spike-mark on my cheek.

"That all you come away with?" he asked.

"That's what started those festivities," I said. "Hey, I'm not the violent type, Satchel: I'm a pretty stand-up guy. You may not believe me, but it's true. That bastard got me mad."

"And then you got a lot of other people mad."

"Maybe so; but who is this Leon Latortue, anyway? He a friend of yours?"

"Never saw him before; but then he wasn't Leon. Leon Latortue is our new centerfielder. He arrived late and only entered the game when you came to bat. Said some white guys tried to hold him up outside the Stadium. Then they let him go. The guy that spiked you, hell, he disappeared. Nobody knew who he was before or after."

"Now, you see, Satch, this is the kind of information that is so important to the case."

"What case?"

"The Buster Fenton Case. It wasn't suicide. We believe the kid was murdered."

Looking at me sideways, Paige raised two non-committal eyebrows.

"Gotta be true, Satch," I went on, "or why would that hoodlum kick me in the face?"

I told him what the fake Leon muttered to me. I told him about the adventure on Bedford Avenue. He listened, moving his tongue around in his cheek.

"Who you working for?" he wondered.

"No cops," I assured him. "A private party."

He lowered his eyelids. He leaned back on the bench. I offered him a cigarette, which he took. I took one too, and we shared a match.

"What do you know about a white woman?" I asked.

He shook his head slowly. He dragged on the cigarette, craning his neck and exhaling as if sending the smoke into the overhead branches.

"If I paid attention to every scandal involving some black boy, I don't know but I think I'd know just about too much," he opined suggestively.

So he did know something. Ol' Satch. Just so cool.

"So, then," I continued, "the kid wasn't a gambler or a double-crosser or anything that touched on dirty business. He was a lover. That's it, ain't it? He loved another man's wife, and she was white."

"How much are you getting paid for this investigation?" he asked.

I didn't reply to that. I had no money for him, if that was what he wanted. Instead I told him about my visit to Horace Stoneham, owner of the New York Giants. Perhaps I could get him to add to what was already known among other baseball playmakers. If Jimmy could lure Satchel out of the bar with the truth, maybe I could follow suit. The man loved to be teased. That's why he himself was such a teaser. Of course, another possibility was that he was somehow involved in the murder! One never knew. If that were so, my goose was already cooked. Out at first, trying to steal! In which case, I had nothing to lose now. I felt, however, that Satchel was okay.

"Satchel, what can you add to what is already common knowledge? How does baseball and Leon Latortue's substitute connect with the white babe?"

I was optimistic, counting not only on Satchel's privilege to all the scuttlebutt but also his personal awareness of justice. Surely he must've respected Buster's potential and saw him as successful in the white leagues. I hoped that he was above jealousy here. I hoped he could lean towards my objective. Surely he was the man to see the larger picture, and surely he sympathized with his race regardless of his own personal frustrations at not being first in the Majors. After all, he was already a success.

"Baseball? A white woman?" I said again.

Satchel whistled a bit. If he knew the answer, he was taking his time in telling it.

"Satchel," I began in another vein, "you're a man of great self-confidence. And believe it or not, I appreciate what you did today to calm everyone down--even though I came out looking like a fool. But you are nobody's fool, neither black nor white, and you play to win, am I right? What I mean is, how do I get to have some of that confidence? I need to find a direct and truthful way to Buster Fenton--or his ghost--without mumbling and stumbling all over myself."

"I love baseball," he said offhandedly, taking another drag, "because it is the sport that demands the most in flow motion." The phrase was his own concoction. "See, you have an opponent, and he has a goal, which is to beat you in the game. You have the same goal, which is to beat him. Now, you both enter the game in a flow, and you let that flow take you through until you win or you lose. To win you got to make your flow upset his flow. To lose, you, well, it's the reverse: You let his flow upset yours. This is true for every sport: boxing, basketball, football, soccer, you name it. All of them bring you, once the game begins, into the act of flow motion, a calculated movement from one place to another; calculated, see, to upset the other man's flow."

"Okay," I let him know that I was listening carefully.

"Now, baseball," he continued, "requires the most variety of astute movements from one thing to another in opposition to another thing with its own flow motion: one pitch to one swing, one bend to one ground ball, one stretch to one catch. Every gesture matters, and it is poised against a target with a mind and body in opposition to yours. Know what I mean? To be successful in baseball, you need to go neither fast nor slow but to flow against the other team or single man and in perfect understanding of his power. Then your flow overcomes his. In other sports, there is a flow, of course, but it's a lot simpler. Worse yet, the basketball or football or soccer ball goes bouncing around all crazy and then maybe somebody gets a basket or runs for a goal or kicks the ball past the other player. In boxing there's a lot of dancing around the ring and a lot of missed punches. More instinct than mind there. But when a ball goes haywire in baseball, we call that a foul or an error. To make points in our game we need an elegant precision--and a mind to work at it. Works on both sides. Bat hits ball square, that's a hit; bat hits ball an eensy bit off, that's a pop up--you're out. See what I mean? Same thing with pitches. I studied that before I got good. Same thing with catches, same thing with throws, same thing with running bases. In baseball a man has got to be an expert in flow motion: and that is every minute of the game knowing where, when, and how to act--or not act at all. You got to have a handle on both the positive and the negative. Now, when I threw you that change-up, I was dealing in the negative. But I was still dealing: I knew your strength, and I knew my own. And I knew the possibilities."

"Flow motion," I pronounced.

"That's what I said," he confirmed.

"Then what about billiards? That's a game of many variables, of sharp vision and precise shooting."

"Who are you playing against in billiards?" he countered. "Sorry, but you can't put billiards in the same category. Everything sits still while you shoot. Same thing with golf. That's not flow motion; that's just finesse."

"What about tennis?"

"Or ping-pong? Good, of course, but limited."

"Then what about bull fighting?" I knew he must've taken in some bull fights while playing in the Mexican league.

"That's a good question," he admitted; "You could die if you make the wrong move in that game. But who are you playing with? An animal? Animal got no mind. Animal don't understand the flow."

Politely, I wondered where he was going with this philosophizing.

"Lots of places," he said. "Because I see that you want to master that flow in real life. If so, you need to have your gestures make sense. To do that you need to stand up in the game. You can come to the plate all worried and nervous, thinking about the fans and fretting about whether I'm going to throw a beanball. That's how you lose. You have to forget about fear, if you can. So you can deal with the truth. I can see you want the truth, the truth for yourself beyond all else; that's why you're pursuing this Buster business. But you're still afraid of what isn't there, the untruth. You're afraid of the lie. You're afraid it might come and overtake you in the darkness. Man, you got to stand up in the game. Only then can you consider the flow. And when you flow, you have to consider how the other side flows; they take a bead on what they see as truth too; and it takes a mind to make the muscles act they way they do. A mind, see. No mind, no flow. No flow, no truth. Remember, though: you're not playing with animals. Maybe worse."

He rose as he concluded, unwinding his body with an easy grace; then he flipped his cigarette on the grass and said: "You go find that other mind."

He saw my perplexity. The other mind? What the hell was he talking about?

"The mind is in the head," he elucidated, pointing to his own. "Every team..." and then he seemed to changed his focus: "Well, first you got to stand up in the game." He didn't elaborate. Instead, he looked off towards Jimmy, who'd been wandering about the park. We could see her about a hundred yards off, taking slow steps and glancing up at trees. He nodded towards her. "A woman is the object of every man's flow motion," he offered casually.

Wouldn't you just wish, I said to myself.

"Not just yet. Not her. She's on reserve. She's in mourning," I said. "She's in the negative."

"Sorry I couldn't be of any help," he uttered, saluting me with two fingers,

I sighed, nodding.

"Thank you, Satchel," I said without standing. "You're still my hero."

He smiled. "It was nothing," he said and started to walk away. After ten paces, he turned, just as if he were checking me at first base. "Tell your lovely friend that Satchel will be in The Huntsman until ten p. m. Unless I meet with some other entertainment beforehand."

"She lives in Philly. With her parents," I replied and then hated myself for revealing even that.

"We all did once," he responded. "Then we grew up."

"Bye, Satch," I waved. "See you in church."

"Be careful," he warned. He loped easily away, his hands dangling by his sides. He whistled as he went, going to have a steak dinner with his friends.

Damn, Damn, Damn. That was all that rang through my head. Damn. He knew something about the crime, but he had to be careful himself. Damn. So he had to talk like an oracle, like some wizard surrounded by smoke. Damn. And Leon Latortue was not Leon Latortue. Momentarily, Jimmy stood before me, and I asked her to sit and listen to my account of the interview.

"You know exactly who he meant," she said.

"He meant someone?"

"The mind? Every team has one. The head?"

"Sounded like gobbledygook to me."

"It's Tom Baird, the Monarch's owner! Satchel's boss! You get it?"

I guess I did. Phew.

"What about that Leon?" I asked. "Some connection, right?"

She agreed. Then she added: "I like your sense of purpose. I feel I can trust you."

"I like yours," I replied. "And I trust you."

A little white moth fluttered along and landed on her hand. She studied it a while, then gently blew it off.

I had a hard time holding myself back from taking her hand and kissing it. Instead I inhaled deeply. Yes, it's true: I had to admit it. I'd already begun to see how curiously pretty she was. I must've been blind at first; for here was Satchel Paige looking to latch onto her! But, even so, I think I began to see her beauty once she showed her spirit, once I could see how smart and lively she was--with no fear: ready to stand up in the game, as Satchel said. It's the spirit that makes the face appealing.

"I'm on vacation next week," she said. "It's the slow season for the hotel."

"Funny thing." I didn't believe I could ever lose interest in her, not when she showed her spunk, like this.

"Funny thing," she echoed.

So she proposed to join me on the quest: to go visiting and asking questions, to work with me hand-in-glove. She could always help out when we were, as the Englishman says, in a sticky wicket. Or I could help her. Either way.

The plan was simple. She would stay with Aunt Monique in Harlem. I would travel back and forth to pick her up, and together we would pursue the mystery of Buster Fenton's death. For our own satisfaction. Still, I wondered. What did she know? What did she want, some kind of justice? For herself? Or, as a woman, such as revenge against another woman? A white woman?

"We'll continue to do what we're doing," I concluded.

"Good," she said. "Now let's go find Tom Baird. I know he might hate me for trying to talk Buster out of the Negro League, and I know, if he is somehow involved in the crime, he might prove dangerous to you. But these may be good reasons to confront him head on. He'll see that we're not pushovers."

Dangerous, did she say? Hell, I might get shot right on the spot if he were as bad as he needed to be! Did this girl have any sense of reality? Go find Tom Baird and then get found ourselves, "hanged," as it were, in some Brooklyn basement? I realized that this, this visiting of the Monarch's chief owner, should've been my intention from day one. It was so obvious a move, I stood still for a moment visualizing the man as he sat with a white friend in the box seat in KC's Municipal Stadium. I suspected that Baird was in town for the past few days, following his team and working some business in the East. Why had I blocked this from my mind and only gone to see Horace Stoneham? The answer was fear, irrational fear. Somehow I trusted Stoneham to be upright, probably from his reputation, because I'd never met him. But Baird I did know, and there was, well, I don't what it was, something about him I couldn't feel comfortable with.

For why had Mr. Paige been so cautious?

Jimmy, however, calmed that feeling. She reminded me she'd dined with Baird and her fiancé in Manhattan and saw that the fellow was mild-mannered. He could get mad, perhaps, and shout a bit; but she doubted whether he'd kill us then and there, especially if we surprised him with a visit. Then again, maybe he didn't hate her at all. In fact, she'd seen him at the game today, where he waved at her from another section! As for the danger, since he was a major suspect, well, we'd say we came about Buster's gravestone. We'd ask for a donation. Then subtly we'd bring up the incident of Leon Latortue--or his substitute. We'd see if Mr. Baird would blink. When I mentioned that someone was already out to get me if I didn't mind my own business, and that that someone could be Baird himself, Jimmy reminded me that it was still daylight, and we could make a quick getaway, as we had in Flatbush, if anything appeared suspicious.

We would stay in town for a while; I would take her home late.

For now, it was time to stand up in the game.

We went to call on the man.

CHAPTER SIX

"Standing Up in the Game"

I laugh at myself now, but I have to admit I was scared. Only consider, Tom Baird was a prominent figure in Negro baseball, and he was white. This meant he had a network of friends all over the U. S. He also had what seemed to be bodyguards, notably his second baseman Hank Thompson. Actually, the man should've been the next person after Horace Stoneham that I spoke to about Buster's demise, since Jimmy told me that he'd been negotiating with the kid. But how was I to begin when I knew he was back in Kansas City? Now he was in Jersey City with his team. I'd seen him in the box seats behind the Monarchs' dugout sitting with the fellow he'd sat with in Kansas City. Why hadn't I approached him during batting practice? Fact was, he intimidated me; why, I couldn't say. Deep down I was sure he was behind Buster's murder.

This gentleman had the most to lose if the Negro League went belly up. So why wouldn't he resent Buster's hesitation to sign with the Monarchs? Furthermore, he might have felt betrayed when he'd heard that Buster was playing footsie with Horace Stoneham. And what about the white babe: Was she from Kansas City or back East here? Maybe Baird felt some sort of racial animosity toward Buster once he'd heard about the affair, especially with a woman, possibly, from his home state. And now this business with Leon Latortue or his impersonator, Leon the Spiker, as I prefer to call him: Perhaps Baird personally hired him to warn me against peering into the mystery. How else might that hoodlum have gotten a Monarch's uniform and been put in the line-up? Didn't the boss have to okay that move?

That was another thing. Who told who I was doing this? How did anyone besides Jimmy know I'd been asking personal questions? The janitor with bald head in blue overalls? Life could get pretty weird sometimes; one never knew who was the enemy.

Now, however, it was time to stand up in the game. We needed to face the enemy, if enemy he was, head on. I wonder now if I'd have gone alone, without Jimmy, who Baird had been pleasant with at the dinner with Buster. Probably not.

The guy kept an apartment in a building he owned in Jersey City. I learned this from a call to Toby Hughes, who was a fund of information on baseball business. Toby gave me the man's address, that of a four-story apartment house in a borderline neighborhood, where the mixing of black and white faces didn't seem out of place. Tom Baird owned half-share in the KC Monarchs, the biggest money-making team in the Negro League; but he had other interests too. It was easier for him to do business here in Jersey City, since he dealt with both races all over the country, keeping his home in KC and working a lot in the New York area. He had real estate in Los Angeles and Minneapolis, so Toby told me. He may have had investments elsewhere. But here he was in a modest first-floor apartment, about ten city blocks from that little park.

It was seven o'clock when he answered our ring and admitted us. He had the radio on loud, and we could hear the opening sounds of "Gangbusters": "The only national program that brings you authentic case histories . . . ." And then the siren, the machine gun popping, cops chasing crooks, and then the blast of the police whistle. The title of this week's show was "Appointment with Death." Silently, I hoped that that fate would not be mine or Jimmie's.

Baird's face dropped when he saw us, not because he didn't like what he saw, but in recognizing Jamesetta he knew that ours would be a long visit--long enough for him to miss his "Appointment with Death." His mind registered "girlfriend" and "opposed to signing with KC" and "I thought this was over and done with." He had that I've-had-a-long-day expression on his thin face. He might've told us to return the next day. The way he turned back to look at the radio I could see this was one of his favorite broadcasts. He needed the relaxation after a stressful week, I imagined. But on recognizing Jamesetta, he must've judged that we were serious visitors and decided to be polite.

If he knew me, however, he didn't let on.

He asked us to come in and sit on his living room couch. He turned off the radio.

He seemed a quiet sort. If this was a style that masked the killer, I couldn't say. In his middle fifties or so, he was tall. His face was lean and forthright; he was sharp-nosed with a firm mouth. His eyes were watery blue. I'd call him borderline handsome. He wore a white shirt with the collar unbuttoned and cuffs rolled up on his forearm. He had a down-to-business air about him; but, still, he resembled the small town types who had a secret life in the KKK: I could see him in a white cloak and pointy hood. Otherwise, I'd take him for a Presbyterian minister. He spoke kindly to Jimmy; or was he just oily-smooth?

"I saw you at the game today," he said softly. "I meant to offer you my condolences. Well, let me offer them now." She thanked him.

"I had a lot of respect for Buster," he said; adding oddly, "People say the wrong things, rumors; and business being what it is, strange things happen . . . ." Did that explain away murder? He'd tailed off, looking embarrassed.

He offered us a glass of lemonade, from something only a busy man might concoct: a pitcher of water, with ice cubes and sliced lemons thrown in. He noted we could add sugar if we cared to, indicating a sugar dish on the coffee table. We accepted and scooped several teaspoons of sugar into the drink. He already had a glass of his own.

"Moonbeam Slyder," he said, sitting himself in an armchair opposite us, nodding, "I remember you now. Sure. You stole home on Satchel Paige." He laughed a slight, pleasant laugh, the joke being on Satchel, his off-season business partner in the barnstorming tours. Then he shifted gears. "Okay, this isn't just a social call. What do we have on the table?"

"Leon Latortue," I enunciated.

"Who?" he asked. I repeated the name. "Oh, yeah, right. Just took him on. What about him?"

"Is he really Leon Latortue?"

He looked perplexed.

"I mean," I corrected myself, "is he the man who spiked me today?"

"In that donnybrook?" he asked. "Oh, my. I didn't see that. I had to take a telephone call. Long distance. I was missing in action." He chuckled at his own joke. "I heard about it afterward." He stared at me. "You," he pointed, "you're the one who started it. No, no, no, don't apologize. If he spiked you, well, I can understand your reaction." He rubbed his chin. "But that sort of incident, you know, isn't good for the game."

"Then you don't know," I said.

He shook his head slowly. "I can't imagine," he said, "that anyone could've just jumped into the game, in uniform, to spike your cheek."

"I was wondering if you might look into it," I added.

"As far as I know there was no substitute," he continued thoughtfully, "though this sort of prank wouldn't be new in my experience." He didn't elaborate. "I'll ask my manager." Then he leaned over the coffee table to inspect my wound. "Pretty mean. Hmmm. Nasty. If Leon is responsible, I'll discipline him."

After thanking him, I paused. If he had sent Leon the Spiker to warn me against further detective work, why would he be acting so nice now? Of course he might be trying to find out how much I had learned so far. As we both sipped our lemonades, I could see his eyes narrow as he slowly studied my face. I returned the gesture, wondering where I could go from here. I breathed deeply before deciding. That is when Jimmy suddenly broke her silence with:

"Is it a common occurrence for teammates to pile up around second base? Are the players always so wild and unruly?"

After setting down his drink, Baird clasped his hands and leaned forward, smiling. "The boys have been known to engage in a rowdy sort of humor," he said. "This time it started with a spiking that, well, shouldn't have happened. Evidently, Wyatt"--who?--"was in on the gag, aware I'd been called away:

I had to converse with someone from Minnesota about a post-season schedule in St. Paul. Hmmm." He characterized the spiking as a gag. That meant he suspected some kind of funny business. And who was this Wyatt?

The name seemed to have an effect on Jimmy, who suddenly spilled her lemonade onto her lap. She stood; I stood. Baird stood.

"How could I do that to myself!" she exclaimed, standing and beating at her dress. "Oh, how could I do that! Oh, oh! Mr. Baird, may I use your bathroom?"

Mr. Baird indicated the direction of the bathroom, and Jimmy scurried away. I shrugged at the man, and he looked back embarrassed.

"I'm still confused," he said. "Did I say something that upset her?"

I replied with another shrug, and while he kept staring at me, I thought it would be a good time to proceed with another point of my inquiry, especially now that Jimmy was out of the room. So I mouthed the words "white woman." When he squinted as if to hear me better, I whispered, "White woman."

He returned a look of guarded, or was it fake, puzzlement. I didn't know how to follow up this line, so I looked back over my shoulder to see if Jimmy would return. Then I turned to him again and blurted, "Was Buster seeing a white woman?"

His eyes opened wide at this. He looked down and to the side. The words seemed to frighten him. Then he began to shake his head. He looked up at me and kept shaking his head. He didn't answer me. And now Jimmy returned to the room.

"I'm so sorry, Mr. Baird," she said. Her dress had a large wet spot down the center. She, too, assumed a sheepish, embarrassed silence. Now we three all stood in a circle, not speaking for a while. We could hear the large floor fan by the window whirring in silence. Then Baird cleared his throat and seemed to motion towards the door. That's when Jimmy, ignoring the gesture, walked to the window to dry her dress there, patting it down before the large floor fan that whirred and whirred.

"That was no gag, Mr. Baird," she said, looking out through below the lifted shade. "After that fake Leon Latortue spiked Moonbeam, he told him to be careful or the next time it would be his nose!" She continued to slap the wetness on her blue dress.

"He threatened you?" the man turned to me.

I felt as if I visibly began to reel. I suddenly understood the danger I had placed the two of us in. If the man had sent this hoodlum to get to me, I realized how close we were to death just standing there in the room with him. The idea unnerved me as much as Jimmy's casual attitude, as if she might say anything to set the hounds on us. My mouth dried up; I couldn't answer him. But I had committed myself: I was standing up in the game; I couldn't leave now.

"Yes, he threatened him," said the wide-eyed Jimmy, turning back into the room. She was pert and proud now, and the spot on her dress in some measure disappeared. It was the little success of her drying efforts, it seemed, that set her going.

Baird darted his pale blue eyes back and forth between her and me. I couldn't decide if he was scared or angry.

"I will definitely look into this business," he said.

"Thank you," Jimmy said; "I think you will find that this business is very serious."

He took a long look at the girl. "You were Buster Fenton's fiancée," he nodded. "You were going to be married next month."

"Next summer," she corrected him.

He acknowledged the correction, coughing into his fist. Surely, he knew about Buster's other woman. Was he in on the murder or what?

"You didn't want him to sign with the Monarchs, now, did you?" he wanted to establish this fact.

"No," she admitted.

"Afraid he'd be moving around the country too much. You and I," he added, "were among the last to see him alive."

Among? I remembered Jimmy's telling me about Hank Thompson being at the dinner. Any others?

She nodded. He nodded, too, sticking his hands into his pants pockets. Then with a quick movement he began to pace, his chin downward. He paced around the entire living room, stopping briefly to glance out the window. He looked at Jamesetta several times, then looked down again. Could he have given Buster a lot of money? Could he have planned to kill Buster once he realized that Buster was going with the Giants? Anyway, it all got back to Leon the Spiker, I concluded. If he'd hired Leon to get to me, then he was guilty. It was simple logic. On the other hand, who was left? Damn, did he act suspiciously!

Who knows if he wasn't planning to have us murdered on our way home!

He stopped pacing. "Buster had his chance. You were there. I offered him a big contract. You know the amount," he stated. "He wanted to think it over."

"You may think that I influenced him against you," she said. "But Buster was independent. He was a thinker. He weighed things."

"Well, apparently he played both ends against the middle," Baird stated, gesturing with his hands out of his pocket.

At this moment I seem to have lost all my reticence. I suddenly felt I'd have nothing to lose if I went on the offensive. I jumped in and said that I supposed that he, this big-time owner, didn't seem to mind that. It gave him a chance to grab Buster for the Monarchs. "I don't understand why you, an owner in the Negro League, would cause a Negro player to default on his contract with the Bluebirds so that he could play on the Monarchs? Aren't we all in this together?"

Now he raised his voice. I'd gotten him in a tender spot. "I would never ask a player to break his contract with another team in the league!" He paced again. "But, truth is, Buster never had a contract with the Bluebirds. They paid him on a game-by-game basis: fifty dollars a game. He had no contract for this season. And I offered him a contract for next season!"

He paused, shoving his hands back into his pockets. He shook his head from side to side.

Plausible, I guessed. When I glanced at Jamesetta, she shrugged. She had no idea.

"You can blame Horace Stoneham for luring Buster away," he said weakly. "We're all aware that the Giants wanted their own Jackie Robinson. So Stoneham courted Buster. According to my sources, he offered him what I was prepared to offer him. To play for the '47 season. He'd start right now with their triple-A farm team here in Jersey City."

"But how did you know to follow him here?"

"When he didn't play the next day in KC, I put the word out, and I was told that he skipped town. I put two and two together, hoping there might be some hitch in the Giants' offer."

"Who did you ask?" questioned Jimmy.

"Your catcher," he directed the answer to me with a short laugh. "Herman Glove. He came to us." He stopped, picked up his glass, and sipped his lemonade. "He told us Buster had run out on the Bluebirds. He was curious to know what I intended to do about it. He told me all about Buster's salary arrangements with Uriah Holding. And he knew all the about the boy's communications with Horace Stoneham. He asked me to bring legal charges against him, against Buster, to keep him on the Bluebirds. Ha. Herman was loyal to the Negro League. He didn't want the white Majors to buy out Buster the way they'd bought out Jackie Robinson."

Good old Herman. Just one step too many, as I saw it.

"So," he continued, "I figured, hell (and here he looked apologetically at Jimmy), the kid's future is up for grabs. Baseball may be a game, but you can't play big league ball unless you're making money from it. Any idiot knows that. I was sure that that consideration was the reason for Buster's departure for New York. But he didn't come here looking for me"--this, significantly, to Jimmy--"and so I figured rather than let Stoneham get him easily, I'd put in my bid too. Why not?"

I nodded noncommittally. "So, then," I wondered, "what do suppose happened?"

"When?"

"When Buster failed to call you the next day? After your dinner at Helen's with him and Miss Kelly here?"

"Oh." He scratched his chin. "I can't say. Bad things happen to young fellows, sometimes for reasons that are hard to figure." After taking another sip, he glanced from me to Jamesetta and back again. His eyes seemed to have gotten bigger. Again I heard the large floor fan whirring in silence. Soon Jimmy's intense stare began to get to him. He wavered. "You might ask Hank, though. Hank Thompson? My second baseman. And chauffeur. He dined with us that night. He may have been the last to see Buster alive, I believe." He looked regretful, as if he shouldn't have offered this.

"Miss Kelly has told me," I began, "that Buster was not, to her knowledge, a gambler or a saloon habitué."

The man smiled weakly. "No, no, if Miss Kelly says that . . . ." But his ending trailed off like beer from a knocked-over glass. Why was he shuffling this off on Hank Thompson?

"As practically his roommate, I can confirm . . . ." I filled in the pause.

"Murdered?" he suddenly asked. He eyed the two of us. "You imagine he was murdered? Is that why you two came here?"

"The evidence. . . " I started to say.

"There is no evidence," he interrupted. "I've spoken to the police. Nothing. Nothing, except that Buster Fenton was found dead in that basement in Brooklyn. There's no evidence beyond the fact that he was no longer alive. Miss Kelly, I apologize if I sound harsh."

She smiled without showing her teeth.

"But the manner of his death," I persisted, "was hanging."

"So they said."

I told him that Jimmy and I visited the apartment building in Brooklyn. I described the basement, noting that I had seen no sign of any recent activity and no place to loop a rope. Not that I had seen the whole basement, but still . . . . He kept nodding rhythmically. Even as I finished, he continued to nod. Had he known that we'd been there, asking questions, I wondered to myself.

"Yup," was all he said, as if to himself. The floor fan by the window whirred and whirred. He checked his watch. He grabbed for his glass of lemonade that he'd placed back on the coffee table. Only the lemon slices lay in it. He put it down again. He looked directly at us but didn't speak.

"And you suppose Hank Thompson might know more?" I asked.

"Might," was all he answered. He looked from Jimmy to me and back again.

We took the hint and turned to go. Baird lifted his trousers by his belt. With a lopsided grin, he gestured towards his radio. "Guess I missed the whole of 'Gangbusters,'" he said. "But that's okay. This was more important. And now there's Paul Whiteman's 'Saturday Night Serenade' for half an hour. Actually, I wish it were 'Amos 'n Andy.' Those fellows are a scream."

I told him I agreed.

"Even if Buster Fenton didn't meet with a natural death," he spoke in a near-whisper, "there's not a damned thing we can do about it now." He looked apologetically at Jamesetta. "No proof. And now he's buried."

Jimmy thanked him for the lemonade.

"A pleasure, miss," he replied gallantly. He was glad that we'd decided to leave. "If there's anything I can do . . . maybe make a contribution towards the gravestone . . . let me know. Buster would've been a great ballplayer."

"No proof," I echoed his previous remark.

"No proof," he said, shaking my hand. He paused. "I will look into this business of Leon Latortue."

I thanked him, and we left.

I noticed, though, that he couldn't wait to get to his radio. Or was it the telephone that stood next to it?

Once outside and a block away Jimmy laughed, a harsh-sounding cackle, almost as if the joke were on the world, including us. Had she enjoyed this experience? "We found out everything we wanted to," she said, "but still nothing for sure. It was like hearing voices through a wall."

"And then hitting our heads against that wall."

"We're still alive, Carl," she smiled.

"That's one good thing."

So she too thought we might be risking our lives in visiting Tom Baird. And she was the one who made the suggestion in the first place! Seriously, we could've walked into a roomful of thugs. But all we found was a soft-spoken middle-aged man drinking lemonade and listening to "Gangbusters." So I suppose it was kind of funny. I'd stood up in the game, all right, and it was as if the pitcher walked me. I wasn't sliding into nothingness but flowing with the motion. It didn't feel that dangerous. And yet I couldn't help wondering what was on the pitcher's mind.

Jimmy, too, must've been preoccupied, because the longer we walked the more her mood changed. She grew silent as the warm evening grew darker and the people and the buildings and the trees along the street turned into grainy silhouettes. I also grew silent. Her mood must've been catching, for I began to fret about the future. Where was I going with my career as a ballplayer? Where was I going with all this detectiving? Where was I going with her? Then I had that scared, empty feeling again, sensing that at the bottom of everything, everything ever said and done, there was no meaning, just movement and talk, pain and pleasure, and then more movement and more talk. And for all this fuss, people, black and white, had to suffer in their own peculiar style; laugh, too, but mostly suffer, and suffer not knowing anything was real.

People also had to eat. We stopped at a diner for a hamburger and french fries. Hungry and tired, I imagined Jimmy was too. I proposed that she spend the night here in Jersey City at a woman's rooming house, Mrs. Hargrove's, not far from mine. It would be two dollars, which I offered to pay. Jimmy could telephone the drugstore near Aunt Monique's and ask the druggist to notify the little lady. She was over twenty-one, wasn't she? To my relief, she agreed.

We could sleep all the next morning, or if she wished I would take her to the African Methodist-Episcopal Church near my rooming house. She opted for sleep. I was glad for that, too. Her reward would be a box seat at tomorrow's double header.

Sunday was overcast and gray. The games were nothing spectacular. We lost 2-1, then won 3-2. I managed to steal a base. That steal was the only significant aspect of the doubleheader: It was my last one in baseball. The last one. I guess it had significance only for me. At least Jimmy had seen me run. But I didn't realize the end was so near until the events of the next few days.

Afterwards, at Hannah Hughes' invitation, we had supper with her and Toby and the girls, eleven and nine years old. Except for Hannah's polite inquiries about Buster's baseball career, the dinner conversation proved dull. The children stared at Jamesetta without a word. She herself was oddly quiet. Toby, who resented Buster's death, since it deprived him of Horace Stoneham's five-hundred-dollar scouting fee, seemed to blame the fiancée; so his words were also few. But I was worse than all of them; for I couldn't stop thinking about how Toby had used the same words about keeping my nose clean, only a few days before Leon used them. Had Toby been part of discussion among those scoundrels to devise a way to get me to mind my own business? The day had gotten me so tired I couldn't fake being friendly.

After a dessert, then, of tapioca pudding, Jimmy and I said thank you and then goodbye and started for Manhattan.

On the train to the ferry we stayed lost in our speculations. Jamesetta was moody and contentious. We spoke only to disagree: about baseball, the weather, and the right way to serve tapioca, hot or cold, with her contending, as well, that Hannah's dessert lacked some ingredient.

I was satisfied to think my own thoughts. Tom Baird, it seemed, was a fellow with a secret. Behind his outward appearance as an ordinary guy, something inside made him edgy. What was it? And who was this Wyatt? Did he have an interest in the KC Monarchs? Could there be a connection between him and Leon the Spiker? Was Wyatt the other white guy sitting with Baird when I stole home plate in Municipal Stadium in KC? As I noticed, Jamesetta had reacted to the name by spilling lemonade on her dress, but I hesitated to ask for more information, given her mood and my likelihood of chattering too much and making reference to a white woman. Still, I wondered how much she knew about him.

Then I considered Buster and his connection to Baird. Crazy as it seems now, I even wondered if he was the Monarch owner's long lost son, his little black boy in the woodpile, about which he felt some embarrassment. For why did the man follow him to New York and work so hard to sign him to the Monarchs? Then, again, why hadn't he signed Buster before the Bluebirds found him? Why was he so polite to Jamesetta in his apartment just now? Why all this pacing? What uncomfortable emotion did hold within his breast? Questions, question, questions.

Foolishly, I mentioned this idea to Jamesetta, adding that scuttlebutt around the locker room that Buster'd had a white daddy. I alluded to his coloring, his blue eyes, and his brown wavy hair. Jamesetta acted as if I'd insulted her. She didn't answer at first, just huffed a little. When she did reply, she dealt in sarcasm, of that off-putting kind I'd heard in Philadelphia as she spoke of the Negro League.

"Didn't you notice his mother?" she said liltingly. "High yellow?" She went on in a snide rant about the hypocrisy of color distinctions. I couldn't disagree, but I couldn't listen either. I closed my ears and remembered playing ball in Santo Domingo, where I heard one Dominican razz another about how the fellow lacked white forebears, unlike himself. "We're all mulattoes here," the other guy hit back at him in a hard whisper. He had to whisper because in those days the dictator Rafael Trujillo had set out to make all Dominicans white, one way or another. In fact, I thought I heard a note of racial pride under that comeback. There was nothing wrong with being a mulatto: How could there be? Why couldn't we all forget the fancy name-calling and also the meanness that went along with it? What's in a word: boy, oh, boy. Some mad scientist should invent a word-laundry, one that would wash all the dirt and high falutin' nastiness out words. He would make a million.

So Jamesetta and I agreed on the basic principle; but still we sat there on the bus at odds with each other. By now she'd gone into another rant about Tom Baird's reputation for fairness.

"Do you imagine," she insinuated, "that he had any color sensitivity when he hoped he could listen to 'Amos 'n Andy'?"

I rolled my eyes.

"Answer me." she demanded.

I shook my head. By now she'd gotten me distracted and thinking about Glove's rainbow list of Negro colors: something he'd gotten from reading "Ebony" magazine. I tried to picture in my brain the colors the words defined: they were "smoke," "cinnamon," "chocolate," "cream," "golden," "pecan," and "coffee." I got frustrated matching faces and colors; so I replied finally but thoughtlessly that Baird's favoritizing that radio program showed the he enjoyed Negro performers.

"Negro performers?" she said with rising voice, cocking her head sideways.

"Well, personalities," I answered, modifying my observation. I realized, of course, that Amos, Andy, and Kingfish were played by white actors. But still, regardless of their color, they represented the black race, and everybody loved those characters! What did the actors' color matter? Nobody could see them: They were voices on the radio!

"If you're satisfied with that," she said turning away.

"You take what you can get," I said. "More's coming every day."

"You're an optimist."

"And you're a strange one" I came back. "If you worry so much about Negro integrity, how come you were so dead set against the Negro League?"

She kept her face averted without answering.

I tapped her shoulder, but she she ignored me.

Would she ever be able to get over Buster Fenton, I wondered. And how would she feel once she knew about Buster's other romantic interest?

However, it wasn't love that occupied her: She'd been ruminating on the murder case.

"If you remember," she said, looking out the bus window, "Mr. Baird had a friend with him in the Stadium today."

"Wyatt?"

"Him," she said. "Black hair, parted in the middle, greased back. He kept smoothening with both hands. He seemed restless. He looked at me as if he knew me."

"He stared at me too," I remembered. "Sad, strange eyes. Baird's bodyguard?"

She didn't answer but continued to stare out the window.

"I don't know," she almost whispered.

Baseball suddenly seemed to be indeed a dangerous game. There was the natural rowdiness among the players; but then there was the cut on my cheek; and then there was the death of Buster Fenton--and nobody willing to provide answers for it. The ball field was, in a sense, surrounded with gamblers and gangsters; every now and then there was a remnant of the KKK; and there was Leon the Spiker warning me to keep my nose clean. On the other hand, I needed to remind myself, there was the beauty of the sport, the fun, and the fame. How much of the bad would I be willing to take for the right--I should say, anyone's right--to play in the Major Leagues?

CHAPTER SEVEN

"Moonbeam in the Underworld"

It was night as we crossed the Hudson River from Jersey City. I thought of Satchel's phrase "flow motion" as the ferry's engine pushed the boat against the south-moving current, one flow against another. The ferry had a "mind"; the river did not. High clouds obscured the stars, but the city's architecture formed a mighty fortress-like silhouette against the dark sky: that impressive outline to me always a picture of human possibility. For if all this cement and steel could be flung up against the empty heavens in less than fifty years, what could not be accomplished by men who sat down to think and then got up to do? Men and women, I should say: I looked to my side at the delicate and determined Jimmy leaning against the cold, green metal railing and gazing at the same marvel, a marvel that the ferry, in its flow motion, rocked forward to minute by minute as we approached the looming buildings, leaving New Jersey behind.

A calm descended upon us in the river's breeze. Feeling intimate, I spoke to her of my failure to make the '36 Olympic track squad. There were no Olympic Games in '40 and '44, thanks to Adolph Hitler, the man who made the '36 Games a program for Nazi racial pride. Word was that he'd refused to shake Jesse Owens' hand when our boy had won his races; then I also heard that the Führer simply hadn't shown up in the stands that day. Whatever the reason, Jesse'd come out looking good--for all of us. It was a pleasant thought.

I put my arm around Jimmy's shoulder. She let it rest there until we docked in the slip at Liberty Street. I considered whether she accepted this gesture as a touch of consolation or a confession of sentiment. But she shrugged it off as we disembarked, following the other passengers onto the street. Off-handedly, I considered my next step.

"Hank Thompson," I said the moment our feet touched the pavement. "I'll visit him next."

"Moving along nicely," she uttered.

I didn't know whether she was being sarcastic or whether she thought we'd made progress in our talk with Tom Baird. Now a good distance from the encounter, I felt serene. I kind of laughed when I considered how hesitant I'd been before visiting this fellow, who turned out to be no threat at all, not personally, just a colorless, lemon-slice-and-ice-water man. I believe I'd been spooking myself unnecessarily. Of course, I couldn't be carefree about his hidden intentions, if there were any, but I enjoyed the moment, hoping there weren't.

Yet who knows what a nice person will think and do behind your back? Yeah, what was Baird's edginess all about? For the moment, I didn't care.

Some other time for that, I thought.

I spoke lightly of the visit all the way to Harlem on an empty IRT, rushing noisily through the nighttime of the subway tunnel in the eeriness of its artificial light. Jimmy, however, didn't show any sympathy with my relaxed mood; she sat quietly, staring out the window. It was nearly ten p. m., and station after station passed by in Sunday night solitude. Monday was the next day, when everyone would return to work and start the week all over. As we ascended the station steps and walked the streets over to Lenox Avenue, with the asphalt on those streets black and shiny under the avenue street lamps, we saw scant illumination in the apartment windows. The growl of a distant bus's engine rising and falling provided the only noise. When that faded, only the little clap-clap of our own shoes echoed on Harlem's lonely sidewalks.

As we reached the stoop leading up to Aunt Monique's door, Jimmy turned to me and said, "Perhaps we shouldn't see each other for a while."

Surprised and dumbfounded, I just nodded "okay," searching her eyes for a reason. I'd thought that we had an investigation going, and now this? Who was she afraid of: not me, not Baird, then who? It was too late to stand out in the street and argue. But, man, was this a turnabout.

"It'll be easier," she explained, though that was no explanation.

"Fine," I said and walked away feeling as if I'd been kicked in the stomach.

My next encounter was something I didn't expect and much more serious than the fickleness of a woman-- and much more brutal than a lemonade chit-chat. I thought I'd have an easy time returning to Jersey City, but trouble started after I left Jimmy, with nothing more on my now-puzzled mind than getting back to the subway station where we'd exited. Soon, however, I had the uncomfortable feeling that I'd been followed. How strange it was to confront men in the white world who once seemed awesome and then fret over whether I'd be able to walk a few blocks out of this colored neighborhood to the train station. I peered dimly around for a taxi. Suddenly two characters appeared from nowhere, standing on either side of me at the curb. When I took one step into the street, the two moved around and stopped my progress.

"You one nigger wanna die young," said one of them.

"Yeah," the other agreed, testy-like, as if he'd gotten the idea first. The two looked at each other, then back at me.

Racial sympathy, I judged, was not their outstanding characteristic. They were tall, strong-looking, and menacing, both in long-bodied sports jackets and wide-brimmed felt hats slanted down on one side. They wore slacks stylishly baggy, pegged at the ankle, and long, pointy shoes. Both had one hand in a jacket pocket, the other free, and both moved in similar ways: In the dark I couldn't see a difference between them. They each had foxy-thin mustaches. They didn't seem particularly intelligent, but in their presence I felt suddenly paralyzed. Might I be able to dash down the street, making a getaway? These two would never have been able to catch me, not wearing those banana-shaped leather shoes under those floppy pantaloons! But just as I prepared to run, one of them lifted his hand from his pocket to show a pistol, which he jammed into my ribs. I decided not to attempt escape, fearing that a bullet from that hard-edged barrel might find its way into my back. I was daunted by their meanness, and too tired as well, to take the chance. Then the darkness itself seeped into my heart.

Was this how Tom Baird got back at me for my visit?

"What's up?" I asked, trying to keep my teeth from chattering; it seemed that the evening had grown quite cool. "What can I do for you gentlemen?"

"You can shut your big mouth," said one.

"And you can come with us," said the other, as if competing with his sneering, mustached, zoot-suited twin brother.

Just then a car prowled down the avenue at five miles an hour and stopped--a long, black La Salle, one of those twelve-cylinder models from the 1930s: It had survived the war, probably hibernating in some Harlem garage during the gas rationing and now rehabilitated to proclaim a gangster's self-importance. None of the newer cars, even if you could find one to buy in 1946, was half so elegant. Or scary. In fact, it might have once been owned by a mortician, and why not, for I sensed it was going to take me to my funeral.

"Get in," ordered one thug.

"Fast," said the other, improving on the attitude.

I sat in the middle of the back seat. The two joined me, one on either side, fitting tightly against me with their wide shoulders.

"Now, you be a good boy and close your eyes," one advised.

"You a little tired anyway," drawled the other, touching my ribs with his gun barrel.

Eyes closed, I rode in total darkness. The excursion lasted five minutes. As we parked, I was further advised to keep my eyes closed, and I did. Assisting me from the La Salle, the two led me up thirteen stairs and through a double-door entrance (I could feel the edge of the unopened door against my left shoulder). Once inside I was told I could open my eyes. The two goons then escorted me down a corridor to another set of double doors, which one of the pair knocked on three times then once. As the doors rolled apart, we entered.

Behind a wide, handsome mahogany desk, I saw a hulking fellow come around the front of it, then sit back slightly on the edge. His presence filled the large, dimly-lit room: Hard-faced, a good six feet tall, bulky, he was about forty, confident and intimidating. He seemed familiar, yet I knew we'd never met. As he continued to glare at me, I saw it in his eyes: He resembled Buster Fenton. He was what Buster might've come to if he'd lived another twenty years and gotten mixed up in the rackets! And gotten fat on them. And took money from poor people. And killed anyone who tried to get richer than he--who came across his flow. Not Tom Baird, but he could've been Buster's daddy!

He'd removed the tan lightweight jacket of his three-piece summer suit; he wore his tie pulled away from his unbuttoned collar, his sleeves rolled up. Once set against his desk, he crossed his arms, indicating with his index finger for me to sit in a high-backed armchair. As I did, the two thugs came and stood on either side. But the boss man jerked his head one way and then another, and they faded back to stand by the double doors.

"Who am I?" he challenged with a hard look, leaning into me.

"You got me," I answered. "I don't rightly know."

"Guess," he ordered.

"Bumpy Johnson?" I offered. The name came into my head like a revelation.

He smiled, nodding.

"You're Moonbeam Slyder," he stated.

I crossed my arms, looked down then up, and nodded. Holding my arms tightly across my chest, I meant to keep down the fear that set my heart beating faster and faster and baffled the rhythm of my breath. At worst I would be totally dead in twenty minutes; at best I'd be only half-dead, lying in the gutter with a punched-in stomach and a razor gash on my neck below the spike wound.

"Heard you stole home plate on Satchel Paige," he commented.

I nodded.

"Is that a yes?" he demanded.

"Yes, sir," I uttered.

"It's polite to speak when spoken to," he said.

"I suppose," I replied.

"You also like to go stealing around on the subway."

I shrugged in a cramped sort of way.

"Appearing in places that are bad for your health," he added. "Like Flatbush."

I stiffened and didn't reply.

"You're not being impolite, now, are you?" he asked.

"I'm just awe-struck, Mr. Johnson," I said. Certainly, it's best to be honest from the start: He knew I'd been to Flatbush and why? This Bumpy Johnson was the scariest kingfish in Harlem--the real thing, not that fool character on "The Amos 'n Andy Show." And he was no one to trifle with. From what I'd heard, he'd killed over a hundred men personally in his day-to-day routine. In the '30s he'd done a stretch in Sing Sing; and when he came out twelve years ago, he offered his services to the Queen of the Numbers Racket, Stephanie St. Clair, some voodoo lady from Martinique who'd had Harlem spooked with her uncanny ways. She was unscrupulous plus. She had white political connections, and she used them. She was so bad herself she claimed credit for the killing of Dutch Schultz, who was himself the ugliest of the ugly in the New York underworld.

Now that I looked steadier at him, I realized that I recognized Bumpy because he'd had his picture in "The Amsterdam News" and I'd seen him on Lenox Avenue once, just strolling along and greeting people as if he were Harlem's mayor. He was a study, so they said: He read books of philosophy, wrote poetry, and played a shrewd game of chess. He may have had a wizard's brain, but in my book he had a devil's soul. You tell me which is more important, soul or brain? His true element was violence and ill-gotten wealth: copper and nickel and the little ounces of silver from the desperate coins of ordinary black folk--contributions to the daily numbers game. With the Queen of Darkness now retired, he was King of Harlem's Gangland--a Hades in his own Underworld. His operation raked in tens of thousands of dollars every day!

"Awestruck?" he laughed. "Awestruck in the presence of Bumpy Johnson? Why, Moonbeam, I hear that you're an intelligent man. You should have better sense than to be awestruck in the presence of a mere mortal."

"All the same, sir," I said.

"Right," he agreed, with what I'm not sure. By now I'd lost thought of Tom Baird. All I could question within myself was whether Buster had come afoul of Bumpy in some sort of betting deal. And was it indeed Bumpy who'd killed Buster? It seemed more than certain. Else why'd he be so anxious to come down hard on me? Of all the murderers to choose, Buster had to choose this one! And of all the players to defend I had to choose Buster!

"We do have serious business to discuss," Bumpy continued. "But before we smear the night with unpleasantness, there is one thing I need to ask."

What to do, what to do. What else could I do but appeal to this man's racial loyalty? So I proposed that since I was merely inquiring after Buster's death as a way to give some dignity to the black ballplayer in general, maybe Bumpy could overlook my zeal this time; maybe he could look at me with a philosophical eye as a promoter of Negro welfare, something I was sure he supported along with me. I don't believe I expressed myself too clearly or too well; but in conclusion I said something about keeping my nose clean in the future and not traveling to Flatbush for any out-of-the-way information. Bumpy listened with a half-smile; when I ended, he said:

"The question I had for you was: Do you play chess?"

"Some," I replied, further unhinged by the surprise inquiry.

With a gesture he invited me to join him at his chess table. The chess pieces were white and black--ivory and ebony, as Bumpy told me during the game--hand-carved on special order from Haiti: medieval figures of kings and queens, bishops, knights, castles, and mailed infantry. The detailing was so precise I nearly forgot to be nervous. Surely, he didn't abduct me to play chess with him. No, I believed not. So I began to fret all over again.

"I'll take the white," he said. (Knowing what I know now, he'd made the appropriate choice, since he had the practice of offering himself as a hireling to white gangster money). I took the black with a shrug. "White goes first," he continued. "This is your moment of truth. If you can keep from losing for the next twenty minutes, I'll let you live. If not . . . . You have two minutes for each move. Fair enough?" He moved a pawn two squares forward. "You go."

This was crazy, and not the ideal mental arrangement for playing chess. Moment of truth, indeed. Still, to have played chess with Bumpy Johnson and then died--I supposed there was a weird distinction in that, though not a highly desirable one. Since when did chess become a game of life-and-death? Something felt awfully topsy-turvy here. Just to get myself in a challengeful state of mind, I tried to remember when I'd felt as jittery, since whenever I'd been scared to death in the past I'd found a way to survive, getting past the bad and into the good. Didn't this just happen with the owner of the KC Monarchs? Oh, yes, Tom Baird: the thought returned. What was Bumpy's connection to him?
Put it aside, I said to myself, put it aside.

I recalled, then, my first steal in the Negro League, after my first hit, in my first game. Standing on first base, I became nervous as anything: what to do, what to do? There were thousands of people in the stands watching me. I worried if I should even take a lead. Worried if I might get picked off. As I looked at second base, my left foot felt glued to first. But then, shazaam! I just took off. I ran, slid, and beat the throw from the catcher. The fans all cheered. I stood up, brushed myself down, and said to myself: "Man, you did it." So now I pushed the queen's pawn two spaces forward, removed my finger from the piece, and smiled at Mr. Bumpy--a kind, simple, even dumb-looking smile that told him I was innocent and would never offer him any trouble.

The burly gangster narrowed his eyelids, looking heavily down at the board. Quickly, he repeated his first move, easing the black king's pawn two spaces ahead, next to his other pawn.

"Two minutes," he said, not to me but to one of the zoot-suited thugs, who came forward and turned an hourglass upside down where it sat on Bumpy's mahogany desk.

Jee-sus. Here was flow motion right down on that chessboard. But it was a rigid motion, not fluid, not even true to reality, just a game with set moves. And yet there was a shrewd flow, there was a ticking of time, and there was an end to the game. In this dark atmosphere it was pretty scary.

I calculated I could survive if I lasted nine or ten moves. I could barely think beyond the pawns, knowing that if I lost the game too soon I'd also lose my life. I'd join Buster in that green and golden baseball field in the sky. Oh, yes. But this was no time to joke with myself. Well, there were seven more pawns to move. Then I could jiggle the bishop and the knight a bit; then go castling to get my king out of the way . . . . Maybe, maybe. Lasting twenty minutes might be possible. Nine or ten moves on my side alone! For that's what I'd have to count on, because Bumpy moved instantly as soon as I committed a piece. Either he was a true genius or he wanted me to win, but he took no time to consider his choices; as I saw it, he played sloppily. Through it all, he talked and talked, his chatter in no small way distracting.

"They say it doesn't matter if you win or lose but how you play the game," he began. "But I disagree: Either you play to win, or you don't play at all. To excuse yourself for losing is tantamount to confessing that you don't mind playing poorly, that you really can't get the winning idea, and that you go down to defeat a happy fool. Yet we all know that no one goes down happy.

"They say that I'm an evil character, that I had the brains to be successful in any profession: doctor, lawyer, manufacturer, financier, army colonel, actor, anything. But I disagree." (Every time he uttered this phrase I'd pull my hand back from a move and look up, thinking he disapproved: Then I realized he was only talking). "There was no other profession for me to choose. There was just the rackets. And I didn't choose the rackets. They chose me. The rackets was my doctor's office, my courtroom, my factory, my Wall Street, my World War II, and my stage. Harlem was my stadium, my baseball field, where I could win. Not like you Bluebirds in your rented Roosevelt Stadium in Jersey City.

"Now you question my racial loyalty. Consider my business here in Harlem. They say the Negro will never rise if he don't stop gambling and thieving and slicing up his fellow black man in dark alleys and running after black floozies and bleach-blonde chippies and drinking himself silly and puffing on reefers and juicing on scag whenever he gets feeling low. But I disagree. It's these very sins of the flesh that keep the Negro alive and kicking here in Harlem. And these very sins are my stock and trade, see, providing my fellow persons of color with the joy and the glamor of illicit pleasure. Some of us, of course, have found a way to get rich in this stock and trade: but what's wrong with that? We aren't allowed to participate in the economic ball park of white America. So, instead, we have the sins of the flesh to keep us regularly employed as racketeers, runners, bagmen, and pimps--to put the food in our mouths and the liquor on our lips.

"They say times will change. But I disagree. They will not change for us. I am over forty years old. What's going to change for me? Don't get me wrong. I have no complaint. I'm happy to win like this. You might be too, you know. How much do you make running bases?"

He paused finally. I involuntarily held up my hand to quiet him. He managed to shake me every time I touched a piece, with that "I disagree" line. But now he'd gotten me in a pickle, as his white queen and bishop had trapped my black king in the back row. There were four minutes to zero: two turns of the minute-glass: two turns to survival. But there it was: checkmate in one move. He hadn't played so carelessly, after all. He'd had his strategy, while all I did was advance four pawns and diddled with a knight and a bishop! He'd jabbered me mindless!

"If you ran for me, " he picked up again, "you'd earn two hundred dollars a week! All year round! That's what I'd call running! Salary-wise, you'd beat Satchel Paige to home plate every time!"

In a flash I saw my next move. All I needed to do was sacrifice my knight by putting Bumpy's white queen in check! That could get me over the twenty-minute mark by forcing him to slide his queen out of her risky position. Oddly, though, he refused to see the danger: He pulled his rook into line with the queen and announced, "One more move for you. Two minutes." Why would he allow my knight to take his queen? And, further, how would that be my last move? Then I saw it: my last move! No, no! Yes, yes! For there was his other bishop ready to pounce on my knight! It would have brought my king into check with no way out. Curtains. But now I remembered a desperation move I saw in a sidewalk game in St. Louis. It meant sacrificing my queen by having her crash through his pawn defense and put his king in check. I took my full two minutes. Then off we went, my black queen and I, crashing through: "Check."

Instinctively, he took my queen with a knight. That left me one move and two more minutes of life. Bumpy stood.

"Hold on," I said, "not so fast. I'm not in check."

"Yet. You just bought some time."

"I bought my life," I said, watching the minute-glass before I took his queen with my black rook.

"Checkmate," he claimed, bringing his white bishop into position. So it was.

"But I have two minutes to consider. Rules of the games," I noted. "That would bring me over the twenty-minute mark--twenty-two minutes, to be precise."

"So it does," he agreed.

He rose.

"Listen," he said, "I didn't bring you here to bump you off"--I should note for the record that Bumpy's nickname came from a large protrusion on his head and not from his inclination to murder (one of my problems in concentrating on the game came from fear of looking again and again at the man's head)--"since you're not that big a player." What the hell was I, then? "I brought you here to see how sharp you were, everybody saying that you one smart nigger and all, a reader of murder mysteries, can talk regular like a white man. Well, you are pretty sharp, I can see that, but not as sharp as ol' Bumpy. Now, ain't that right?"

I nodded.

"So you take a lesson from me: You let go of this Buster Fenton thing, you hear?" Though he spoke quietly, he looked hard at me with his black eyes bulging and their whites glowing with heat. "Now, this is the King of Hell talking to you, see; this is Hades. So you take heed. This was nothing, this Buster Fenton thing, just some funning that got out of hand, see, no malice at all. So I hear, and so I believe. Too bad the boy had to die. But we all got to die sometime. You, and I mean you, got to be philosophical about it. Like me. Personally, I am not even involved. Just doing someone a favor. You dig?"

I dug. In fact, I dug real well: Bumpy'd been hired to scare me. Somebody else was in the closet, so to speak, paying him to cover up the crime. My eye focused on Bumpy's white king standing alone in the last row of the chessboard. That white king sure looked like the owner of the KC Monarchs!

"Normally," he continued, "I might take a piece of your little finger as collateral. But I don't believe that will be necessary. I know where to find you."

"Okay," I said.

"Anytime you need work," he added, signaling his associates, "you think of me. No intelligent person need to starve in Harlem," he concluded when I didn't reply.

I kept thinking: "I'm going to live! I'm going to live!"

The two zoot-suiters led me out the front door, advising me to close my eyes. I obeyed. They had the chauffeur in the La Salle drive me around for ten minutes. We were on a deserted dead-end street when they stopped and told me to get out. I did, and they did. I thought this was bad enough, marooning me here, somewhere in Washington Heights, as I suspected; but there was more to come. One of them held his pistol for me to see, and the other thug approached me. He punched me in the stomach, then clocked me in the jaw. I staggered back, still bent over my gut, not seeing anything for a few seconds but gray fuzz. That's when my brain clicked in, telling me to do what I did best--run.

I leant over and butted full force into the one who hit me. He staggered back into the guy with the gun. Then I pushed my way past the two of them and ran up the street, ducking and twisting at every footfall. Accidentally, I slipped to the ground just as the gunman fired at me. I sensed a bullet whizzing over me and zinging into the brick wall a few paces ahead. That was a lucky fall in one way but not in another, as you'll hear. I rose quickly and kept running. The darkness shielded me from further harm. Still, I ran bent over, zigzagging, and there was no pistol that could trace my motion once I traveled twenty feet and more--not on that moonless night. Soon I turned a corner. There'd been only one shot. And now I couldn't hear any footsteps clacking on the pavement behind me. So I slowed down but kept jogging until I'd gone any number of streets this way and that, coming at last to the Madison Avenue Bridge over the Harlem River. I sat down under the large blocky stanchions to rest. Feeling safe, I decided to stay there till morning, maybe sleep some. Of course, I didn't sleep much.

Why hadn't I run away when the two zoot-suiters first accosted me? The answer was that I was scared but I hadn't yet had the scare scared out me playing chess with Bumpy Johnson! So much so that I was no longer afraid of the dark.

CHAPTER EIGHT

"Jamesetta Comes Clean"

When the sun came up I collected myself and tramped several blocks back into Harlem. Right off I thought of going directly home, taking the subway downtown and riding the ferry over to Jersey City. I wanted to curl up in my own bed and sleep forever. I was overflowed. I couldn't unravel the business with Bumpy Johnson: if he, in fact, was the killer of Buster Fenton; hired to do it or doing it on his own for some cockeyed reason. Or was he merely paid by some white folks to cover up the crime? And who might such white folks be, Tom Baird and company? The more I came clear in the head the more eerie I felt, as if the world was not the world but some foggy illusion hiding a hideous mystery.

Worse yet, as I stumbled along the sidewalk, I felt my ankle give way and realized I'd damaged it in my jolt for life. Limping, then, into the back of a bakery on Nagle Avenue, where I noticed the time was 6:14 a. m., I bought a nickel cheese bun to kill the bitter taste in my mouth. The bun would have to do since I didn't carry a toothbrush. When I tried to bite on this soft, doughy pastry, I found I could barely chew. My jaw ached when opened and closed. One of my teeth was loose on the upper left side; I touched my jaw--swollen. So here I was limping along like a three-legged dog and no strength to chew a bun, much less a bone. I wouldn't be able to eat decently for another week; or play ball. So much for Bumpy Johnson's contribution to Negro employment.

So much for my interest in the Buster Fenton Case.

So much, too, for Jamesetta Kelly, with her moods and her ruminations and her blurtings and strange gazes and sudden decision to avoid me. Who could figure that babe out! Out of my league. Besides, I told myself, I never thought much of her anyway. I must've been kind of stupid, taking her to ball games and showing off running bases. No more of that for me.

I was through, beaten, trounced, stomped on, and knocked cold. Yeah, I'd stood up in the game and pretty much got bean-balled. I was down.

Nevertheless, and hardly by my own design, my limping feet led me onto Lenox Avenue, where I struggled down to 129th Street, lame-dogging it over to Aunt Monique's; and there I rang the bell. I was not entirely clear in the head; I just needed to rest, and it being still early this was the easiest stop to make before going home. If Jamesetta wanted to avoid me, all well and good. She could walk right by me; I wouldn't say a word. I'd been deluded by her personality: She wasn't good-looking at all. She'd complicated my life more than I could bother with, and she was plain. Today I was through: I was bushed and calling only on her aunt.

The little lady answered the door with her hand on her cheek.

"My, my," she said, "you have had a hard night. Come in, come in."

I entered.

After chipping at the block of ice in her frigidaire, Aunt Monique fixed me a cold pack, filling an orange rubber water bottle with ice chips. She informed me that Jamesetta was now in the bathroom, where she'd run when she saw me at the door. I lifted my eyebrows and shrugged, as if to say that it hardly mattered to me. Smiling her small smile, she began making breakfast. She was little, as I mentioned earlier, a thin creature with prematurely graying hair. She wore a white-and-black uniform dress and thick-heeled shoes: a mousey woman with quick hands, who always knew the right thing to say and do. Perhaps she was forty years old, yet I felt that she was my aunt also. When she wasn't wringing those little hands and muttering, "Too bad, too bad," they fluttered about the kitchen, all over dishes and pans, and all over her face too, as if to hide herself as she worked. She took sneaky looks at me, though. She spoke hardly a word, except for that muttering, so that I found myself apologizing for the early hour, my raggedy condition, and my lack of hunger.

"I understand," she said. And, "I see you need some sewing. I can fix those tears in your clothes. Too bad, too bad." She indicated the tatters in my shirt and a hole in the knee of my slacks.

She comprehended that I'd gotten mixed up with vicious characters. What else could've put me in this beat-up condition? And it wasn't that she herself hadn't been exposed to life's dangerous side. She had.

Her husband, Wiley Maynard, had died five years before; in fact, his body was never found: not that anybody spent much time looking. So Jamesetta told me later. Aunt Monique heard through the grapevine that Uncle Wiley was knocked off by gangsters in lower Manhattan; and she imagined that his corpse was tossed into the East River, weighted down with cinder blocks. She might've let it go, but the word was also that Wiley'd had a lot of money, maybe in a bank somewhere, about ten thousand dollars; and so she'd gone to the local police station, the old minister at the Abyssinian Baptist Church, and then a white lawyer. All with no satisfaction. Nobody could find Uncle Wiley or his money. (Who knew if he wasn't still alive, I wondered, somewhere in the Caribbean?) Naturally, her refrain became, "Too bad, too bad."

In this connection I later noticed an empty picture frame on an end table in her living room. I discovered that this once held a photo of Uncle Wiley that got ruined when a midnight intruder knocked it over, broke the glass, and wrinkled the picture. The glass had blood on it; so maybe he'd cut himself and run out again. Though Aunt Monique couldn't show the photo anymore, she didn't have the heart to put the frame away; so there it stood, missing her lost husband.

She kept Mr. Maynard's clothes in a large armoire in her bedroom. Jimmy later explained about the picture frame and showed me this closet, with its huge mirror, after Mrs. Monique went off to work: as a chambermaid in a hotel on 2nd Avenue and 51st Street. Her aunt kept the man's three pair of shoes polished and neatly arranged at the bottom. Jimmy explained that there was more than just sentimental feeling attached to these shoes. There was the residue, you might say, of Uncle Wiley's life of crime. (I'd wonder from time to time if Wiley hadn't had some connection to Bumpy, but I never mentioned this to either Jimmy or Monique.) In one pair, the brown-and-white wing-tipped shoes, Monique had found five thousand four hundred dollars, all in one-hundred-dollar bills: fifty-four one-hundred-dollar bills! If she made one-half of that amount in a year, she'd have believed herself a blessed woman. Till then, she'd never seen a single one-hundred-dollar bill in her life. This discovery had made her inquisitive, and that is when she began to hear about the other ten thousand.

I should say that Jamesetta, once she'd prepared herself for the day, entered the kitchen and sat down to have breakfast with me. She smiled tentatively, then began talking as if nothing had ever been said about my not seeing her again. So I kind of laughed to myself and let it go. Actually, I was pretty happy: It made me feel normal again. So I described my visit with Bumpy Johnson, and watched her eyes grow wide. She shook her head; she sighed, pitying me.

"But how could anyone know that you'd been in Brooklyn asking questions?" she wondered.

"Easy," I said. "Someone must've noticed that I didn't show up in the locker room that rainy day. When word got back to Bumpy that two colored folks were in that apartment house, poking around, well, there it was."

"Hmmm."

We didn't discuss a next move or anything about the investigation. She seemed pretty happy too that I'd come by. She noted that Harlem was a dangerous place and that she was glad to see me still alive and breathing. Later, as a way to make me feel at home, she showed me around the apartment and filled me in on family lore.

"You knew all this about the money in the shoes?" I slurred. My jaw weighed about ten pounds, it seemed.

"I am her heiress," said Miss Kelly proudly. "And, yes, I am the only one who knows."

"But now I do," I said.

"Well, so did Buster. But it's still a secret," she whispered. "Can I trust you?"

I nodded. "But why tell me?" I asked. "I thought we weren't seeing each other."

"I'm sorry," she replied. "I'd gotten into a mood."

"Really."

"Really. Am I forgiven?"

"Nothing to forgive."

She smiled. "And now I want you to understand. About my aunt. And also about Buster."

So nice. I surprised myself by how quickly I overlooked the previous evening's farewell. But she seemed relaxed and fresh today. That is, until she mentioned Buster.

She'd been real natural, almost animated, as she showed me around. But now a strange stiffness came into her face as we came and sat again at the kitchen table. She sat up straight and looked important. I'd been relieved that she was sorry about last night. Now I worried that she was getting into some other mode of negativity.

"His gallantry," she said, seeing the look on my face. "He thought he could help her, my aunt." With this she got jittery, her mouth twitching and her hands touching her face. She breathed deeply. I could see it was this Buster-was-great routine again, but with a difference. At first her story was a mass of confusion, of self-delusion, of deliberate, deep, buried-alive sort of lies. And then it all came clean, as if in bright sunshine after rain.

It seems that Buster got involved in Uncle Wiley's case--that is, in a humbug sort of way.

"He'd felt the injustice," she went on, "when he heard the story of the intruder. Even though I warned him that Uncle Wiley had probably double-crossed some Italian hoodlum downtown, Buster felt that something ought to be done and he was going to do it. Still, I tried to convince him that any justice done on behalf of Uncle Wiley could lead to trouble on top of trouble; but Buster disagreed. He knew people who could help, so he claimed.

"When he left the Bluebirds in Kansas City and came back East," she continued, "he intended to sign with the Giants--that is, before Mr. Baird appeared on the scene--and then play the rest of the season in Jersey City with the Giant farm team in the International League. He'd be just like Jackie Robinson with the Brooklyn Dodger team in Montreal. But first he wanted to solve the mystery of Uncle Wiley's bank account. He told me he had a plan. It was complicated. So it would keep him busy. He told me to stay in Philadelphia till everything was accomplished. Not only would he get a contract from Horace Stoneham. He believed that once Mr. Stoneham and he agreed on terms, the man might then help him find Uncle Wiley's hidden money."

And Buster? Going into negotiations with the Giants, with the object of recovering ten thousand dollars somewhere out in nowhere? Was he a Don Quixote, jousting with windmills? Gallantry, yes; but nonsense, absolutely! However, since my mouth wouldn't work, I was all ears. To hear more, I widened my eyes.

Jamesetta sat across from me, her elbows on the white-enamelled kitchen table, her chin perched on the bridge made by her fingers, which kept weaving into each other, as her chin kept moving from side to side. She seemed on the edge of something, something even she was unclear about. I could see it had nothing to do with me.

So Buster was getting Horace Stoneham to find out what happened to Uncle Wiley and his money! What a bouquet of phony-smelling roses this lover boy handed her and she accepted! What had he been doing; what was he after? It suddenly got all very confusing. Obviously, he'd been making whoopee with this white gal--and continuing to do so while in Manhattan. While he kept Jamesetta in Philadelphia. Well, there it was.

I got restless now because her strange mood of yesterday had turned into today's mood of fairyland. Okay, so she didn't want me out of her life. But her brown eyes darkened as she looked upward, shifting from side to side as if to avoid contact. She understood a lot of nothing in her

127

unsettled manner. And she was so serious. Or deliberately lying.

Unfortunately, as she heard it, Mr. Stoneham eventually begged off, claiming he couldn't get his team involved with the New York underworld. Reporters lurked everywhere, listening particularly for gambling or interracial chit-chat relating to sports figures. The last thing Negro rookies in the Major Leagues needed, said Mr. Stoneham, was a scandal, especially if it touched on white women.

"White women?" I questioned, holding my breath.

"Yes, white women. He must've been thinking of Uncle Wiley's girlfriend."

Uncle Wiley's girlfriend?

There was something definitely out of focus here: a white woman, and she was Wiley Maynard's girlfriend? As I listened my heart beat like a tom-tom at a rain dance. But I kept silent. Wasn't it Buster, in fact, who'd been dating such a woman? That's what Mr. Stoneham had confirmed for me! On the other hand, that didn't exclude slick Uncle Wiley from crossing the barrier. Or did this white-woman business slip out in conversation and then got covered with an allusion to her uncle?

And was this white-woman business the reason Buster left off negotiations with the Giants and started in with the KC Monarchs?

But back to the Wiley case.

Apparently, the white-woman business was genuine. Working on the case for about a week, Buster, so Jamesetta continued, unearthed valuable information. He'd gone to a white lawyer, William O'Reilly, who had an office on 92nd Street and Amsterdam Avenue. The man came up with some floozy's identity, a low-level mafioso's girlfriend, who evidently liked sneaking out with sharp-looking black guys like Wiley Maynard. But that was all. He told Buster to forget about everything--everything. But Buster wouldn't. He spent a few nights asking around, discovering that this chippie was an entertainer, a singer in sleazy joints around Broadway. He then reported that when the hoodlum discovered how she'd cheated on him, he threw acid in her face. Then he went for Wiley. No one knows what happened after that. Wiley wasn't around to tell.

Pretty horrible stuff. This could all be true or only some of it or none of it. Could Buster have been killed for getting involved in this business? For asking too many questions? I wondered. My brain was ticking. Buster may have had a basic truth here--about Wiley and his extra-curricular activities--that he decorated with whipped cream and sugar flowers in order to throw Jimmy off the scent of his own forbidden chickadee! While Jamesetta waited for him in Philadelphia! Adoring his greatness from a distance! So that while he'd be her eternal hero, he'd also be the white lady's every-day lover. Every night in New York. Oh, yes. Now I got antsy, wanting to slip away and never tell this girl sitting across the table the strange, unseemly thoughts I had about Buster.

"The color line," she sighed, near to weeping. For Uncle Wiley? And his white girlfriend? She reached for her gift of the glass rose that she'd placed on a shelf in the kitchen when she brought it from home to show Monique. She opened the box and removed the object, laying it on the enameled white table and toying with it gently.

Had she ever imagined that her fiancé-hero Buster ever stepped over that color line? Here he was, handsome, proud, ambitious--and, to my mind, bewitched by some white broad, much like Uncle Wiley's!

I wanted to leave. Instead, my heart still beating and sweat breaking out on my forehead, I asked more questions.

"Had you and Buster set a date for the wedding?"

"As I told you, next June or July," she replied, leaning her head to one side.

"Where would you live then?"

"In New York City, if he signed with the Giants."

"Big if."

"What do you mean?" she asked.

I meant if that white bewitcher didn't put the evil eye on everything good for Buster.

We stared at each other. Then, for all the pain in my jaw, I blurted it out, about Buster's affair. Why? Because I felt helpless and stupid and nearly dizzy over her idealizing the man. More because I hated Buster then for deceiving me as well as her. Also because I was selfish and almost in love with her--I confessed as much to myself--even though she'd begun to annoy me no end. Finally because I couldn't tolerate her self-delusions and because we both needed to have the truth between us as we sat there at the table. "There was another white woman," is how I began, alluding to Horace Stoneham's information, and, "He was a versatile man," is how I ended. Listening, she got sniffly, teary-eyed, but kept a brave front, dabbing her face with a linen napkin. "You were the one true love of his life," I added. With this, she drew her breath smartly in, sitting upright in her chair. She looked away and high, almost toward the ceiling. Something went around in her head, as I could see, and I waited for her to speak.

"Jungle fever," she finally uttered, grimacing at me, then away. She covered her face with her hands. Then with a swift upward motion she stood, awkwardly, lifting the table with her knees by accident and sending the glass rose rolling onto the floor, where it shattered!

Seeing this, she dropped back into the chair and burst into a storm of tears.

I dampened the hotel's monogrammed linens that Monique had brought out for breakfast and swiped up the glass pieces. As I disposed of her broken memento, I waited, leaning against the sink after handing her another linen for her streaming cheeks. Her tears fell for so long I got restless and then sleepy. My jaw ached. I wished I could be lying on the sofa in the parlor. There she could sit nearby and cry her eyes out. At last Jamesetta arose and walked into the parlor, where I followed her. She wanted consolation; she'd almost gotten me to break down in sympathy. Anyway, I sat next to her on the couch and put my arm around her.

Her sobbing subsided, then stopped. She spoke about Buster in another key, full of wonderment and betrayal. "How could he have done that to me? To us? How could he have done that? I kept myself perfect for him," she lamented. After a pause, she looked up and asked me, "Because she was white?"

And so she sobbed again miserably.

"He was young," I said. "Who can tell?"

She dried her eyes with both hands. "I know he was young," she said without emotion. " And conceited. And stupid."

I nodded sympathetically.

"What you've just told me," she confessed, "I've known that too, all along."

My eyes widened, and I breathed deeply. Woman, I said to myself, what a deep dungeon of mystery and confusion you are.

By now, however, my foot had swollen up badly, and I'd grown bone-weary after my restless night under the Madison Avenue Bridge. And now this, this wearisome revelation. Couldn't it have waited? The shock of it fatigued me more deeply. As she needed now to talk about everything she'd kept hidden, I desired only to pass out. But I let her talk, and as she did I became drowsier and drowsier, leaning back and away from her to rest my head on a little sofa cushion and my feet on her lap. Even so, her story entered my mind as if in a dream, like nonsense making sense.

True, Buster and she were engaged; true, too, that they'd planned for a wedding next summer. True as true, Buster had developed a fascination for a white woman. Jamesetta had known all along, and this revelation shocked me the most. How strange the human heart. She put up a proud front, ashamed to tell me until now. But as I told her, she told me. Simple. The situation was like one in a Hollywood movie, one that leaves the ladies sniffling into their hankies during the last ten minutes. Only Hollywood could never make this movie, with the racial mix--the woman so white and the man so black, and each of them betraying their own colors.

The woman's name was Barbara Belsberger, a peroxide blonde in her mid-thirties. She came from Philadelphia, maybe from money, and she'd begun to follow

131

Buster from one semi-pro ballpark to another. An avid baseball fan, she'd eyed the young buck in a game in Pennsylvania and then bought him a drink in a bar afterward. That began this crazy romance. Buster'd confessed this much to Jamesetta after she'd challenged him about his real reason for being in New York when his team played in Kansas City--and after his week-long efforts, so-called, with Mr. Stoneham and the lawyer O'Reilly tied him so much to Manhattan that he never got down to see her in Philly. When they did get together, it was here in town, and Buster'd gotten flustered under her questioning--especially when she demanded to speak to O'Reilly herself--revealing everything and promising to straighten up and fly right and to forget this Barbara Belsberger.

What he'd told her about her uncle was true, he insisted: but he'd met with O"Reilly only once. He did ask around about the gangster's girlfriend and Uncle Wiley. The rest of the time he spent with Mrs. Belsberger.

As it happened, there was Tom Baird, come to New York to sign Buster to the Monarchs. That's when Jamesetta begged him not to, fearing that he'd leave New York, and then once on the road with his new team--Barbara's husband had a small share in the KC Monarchs, Jamesetta discovered--he'd spend time snickety-snacking with his white paramour. And that was what she had against the Negro League! I mean, the Giants spent time on the road, too; but then Buster wasn't in an adulterous relationship with Horace Stoneham's wife!

So Jimmy insisted on going to dinner when Baird invited Buster to Helen's on 110th Street. The Monarchs' boss actually sent a car to pick them up at Aunt Monique's; and Buster behaved proudly at the restaurant. Everything seemed as if it would come out right and happy: a free meal and then goodbye Mr. Baird.

But there was more.

The name of this white temptress's husband was Wyatt. He was supposed to be at the dinner that night along with Baird, he being a part owner in the KC Monarchs. He had money, being a potato chip maker with a wide distribution in

Kansas and Missouri, and that was the man, as it came out, who sat with Baird in the box seats that day in Kansas City. He was Baird's personal friend. He and his wife were estranged a few months before she started in with Buster; the woman had left him to live with her parents in Philadelphia. Well, and this is something we heard later, that week Wyatt had come to New York with Baird and only missed the dinner at Helen's because he was on the prowl for his wife. He'd sent a private detective ahead to locate her, knowing that she and Buster were getting it on here in New York. Supposedly, he missed her and wanted her back.

There it was. The simple mention of Wyatt's name in Baird's apartment had gotten her going, made her awkward and difficult to be with. Made her spill her lemonade on her blue dress.

Amazing it was to hear how much detail Jamesetta had stored in her memory. She'd put Buster through the mill, asking questions over and over again and listening carefully. A woman, if she is bitter and relentless, can get a man to tell her more than he otherwise would. As did our hero. Anything and everything, just to shut her up. But why hadn't the girl told me all this from the beginning? I might've gone at this whole thing differently. And I might not have gotten myself turned into damaged goods at Bumpy Johnson's.

Who knows? Maybe not. And now what?

Tom Baird's friend and partner, Wyatt Belsberger, was the husband of Buster's femme fatale. Judging by Baird's comment on Saturday, I sensed that Wyatt was the one who hired Leon the Spiker to whisper those words to me about keeping my nose clean. Well, well, well. Life got interesting all over again. All this came from opening my mouth and speaking the truth about Buster! The unsavory truth. There was more.

Barbara told Buster that her husband was a kind of maniac. She feared her husband something awful. Wyatt had once given her a bruising that sent her into the hospital for a few days. He'd blackened her eye a few times. Before she left him she got even by tossing a frying pan at him and sending him to the emergency ward with a dented skull! What started that was her discovery that he'd been visiting a cathouse in the colored section of KC. As he objected to her objections, he slugged her; and when she got her breath back, she flung the frying pan. Not very sophisticated folk for all their fancy money.

After Buster joined the Bluebirds, she followed the team through the Midwest and back out to Missouri, only to run into her husband, who she thought was on a business trip in California. Coming into the ballpark, she'd seen him that day while he sat behind the dugout along the third base line with Tom Baird. She'd gone and sat further back and out of sight, so she thought. But he'd no doubt gotten wind of the affair, and set out to find her, and there he was in Municipal Stadium, standing up and eying her with field glasses. She'd gotten hysterical and told Buster, who talked her into skipping town with him and going to New York, where he would meet with Horace Stoneham.

By now I had fallen asleep on the couch, confusing the people she spoke of with Jamesetta and me. I corrected the details later on after a few more conversations on the topic. But for now I slept. I awoke at one o'clock in the afternoon, smelling tomato soup cooking in the kitchen. Rolling over and standing up, I had to go easy on my ankle; it would be sore for a while. I realized I'd better call Toby, letting him know my condition since we had a game tomorrow. First, though, Jimmy had me eat lunch, mostly liquid: soup with buttered toast and a cup of coffee; then we made plans for the day.

She was very lively now. In spite of everything she wanted to go forward.

I called Toby from the drugstore, there being no phone in the apartment. Informed of my sprained ankle, he replied, "You're fired," and hung up. That was Toby, all right, reacting from surprise and frustration. Hell, the Bluebirds wouldn't let a speedy fellow like me wind up on another team. But now that I could barely walk . . . we'd see how things developed.

Meanwhile, Jimmy and I picked up from where we stopped when I fell asleep. The puzzle required only a few more pieces. A short time of thinking and acting might bring us the whole picture. So I asked her how she was disposed to continuing. I'd completely forgotten that I'd quit the case; it'd become too fascinating to let it go now, even with the threats I'd received from Bumpy Johnson and the strong conflicting emotions I felt for Jamesetta. My jaw might be hurting, my foot might be stumbling, but my brain was on fire. Was it life or death? Was I choosing death? Possibly. But the brain's an awfully persuasive motivator: I was ready to go deeper, to enter the flow again--the game was irresistible--to pit myself against the odds at the risk of my life. Yeah, even that. Of course, Jimmy's confession put everything in a different light: It made me brave; and my interest in her got deeper now in spite of everything.

That's right, we would move forward, even with the question of whether she'd be putting her personal safety on the line.

"It's a question of justice," she said. Now, after all those wet tears, her eyes were on fire, and she was rearing to go, exactly at the risk I prepared to assume myself. She'd released herself from her own misery and hurt.

I couldn't deny her. Justice it would be. We decided together--and for each other, even though that question was someways down the road. For now we would try our best to work out the truth in its entirety.

When I commented that Barbara Belsberger used Buster to get revenge on her husband, Jimmy agreed.

"Of course," she said, "but that doesn't mean he didn't find her attractive. Or that they didn't discover an irresistible passion for each other."

"Uh . . . ."

"I no longer," she went on, "have any illusions about him and her."

Good girl, I said to myself, ruminating how I might in the future confess myself in just the opposite way of Buster: how it was she I wanted and nobody else. Or would she now have a mind to hate all men? Or would I hesitate, seeing as how she herself was so complicated a person? Those considerations could wait, though, till after the business with Wyatt Belsberger.

"So," I re-confirmed, "you say they traveled back East together after seeing her husband at the ballpark?"

"Yes, so he told me: It makes the most sense."

She paused. About to cry again, she stopped herself.

"Mr. Fenton, Buster's father, contacted me about his death. He'd been informed by the New York City police."

We wondered then how Tom Baird entered the picture and if he had helped his pal Wyatt murder Buster. For that is what I supposed now, that Buster'd been killed by a jealous husband--and that was, as it turned out, the truth--with help from his close friend, Baird--that wasn't, not exactly.

But where did the police get the idea it was suicide?

Where were Wyatt and Barbara Belsberger now?

What about Hank Thompson, then, Baird's bodyguard: What might he have to tell us, and where could we find him? The web of mystery that weaved its way out in several directions had, as well, a center that drew all the strands together. This center appeared to be Belsberger's need for revenge, instigated by complicated motives of anger and racial bitterness--this last part being all the more twisted since the man had given his wife the same motive for her revenge, and that was his frequenting the colored whorehouse in KC: so that hers took the form of seducing the black baseball hero Buster Fenton! How the mind plays tricks on the heart! A bad business, mostly.

Back to the Baird connection. The man had been polite, too, but also taken up with a secret of sorts, walking around his apartment with hands in his pockets. Hard to figure, that. Had he set Buster up with that dinner at Helen's? Had he helped Wyatt by hiring Leon the Spiker and Bumpy Johnson to cover the crime and get to me? And this seemed far out, but what about a connection with my manager, Toby Hughes? He was easy when it came to money.

We decided that I would get some rest today, sitting on the couch with my left foot in a basin of ice, while I read the newspaper. As I convalesced, Jimmy would return to Jersey

City to seek out Hank Thompson, perhaps by way of finding Satchel Paige first, who could tell her where to find the guy. We thought Satchel, being gallant around women, wouldn't hesitate to help Jimmy, somebody he'd confessed an attraction for on Saturday. So off she went, dressed to the nines, to get money from her bank account, money she'd saved here in New York for her trousseau, and then to ferry over the Hudson to New Jersey.

On a pad she wrote up a number of questions she prepared to ask Thompson about his knowledge of the doings during Buster's last night alive.

I no longer wondered how she, who was such a lady, could engage so willingly in dangerous activity. But she offered an explanation.

"I've had three years of college," she said. "It's given me a view of the world."

How did that mesh with all the bad news about Buster?

"That," she noted, "has given me a view of myself."

I sighed. I remembered the first thought I had of her. What did Buster ever see in her? I'd begun to see plenty. So my question now was: What did he miss?

Finally, before leaving, she set me up nicely in the parlor with the ice basin, towels, little pillows, and "The New York Daily News." When I heard the door shut, I lifted my wet foot from the basin and dried it. I placed it besides the other, unswollen one and lay back on the couch, as I had before. Soon I was fast asleep.

CHAPTER NINE

"Thompson Talks"

Upon awakening I heard the grandfather clock in the corner: tick-tock, tick-tock, tick-tock, gong, gong, gong, gong-- four p. m. Queer how I never noticed it before. Anyway, I rubbed the heaviness from my face and slipped my foot into the basin, only to feel that the ice had melted and the water'd gone cool. Still, the sensation refreshed me; so I sat upright, collecting my thoughts, knowing that I'd probably surprise Aunt Monique when she arrived from work around five-thirty. I stood now, testing the pain in my ankle. The swelling had subsided; I deduced nothing was broken, only sprained, as I'd hoped. However, the pain caused me to sit down again after I'd been to the bathroom and washed up.

To collect myself I read "The Daily News" that Jimmy had handed me. There was not much print beyond a few paragraphs per news item, so I lingered over the news photos, which in this paper were fascinating and dramatic, especially in the centerfold. Today there were shots of a million people crowding Coney Island beach on Sunday; of a large tortoise discovered in the city sewer system; of two couples who'd bought tickets to sail on the maiden civilian voyage of the Queen Elizabeth two months later, in October; and of President Truman inspecting the new air-conditioning at the White House. As I gazed at the countless bodies of Coney Island bathers, my eye kept shifting to the two couples holding tickets to travel on the world's largest passenger steamship, the Queen Elizabeth: four humorous, smiling white folk, the American men sporting English-style derbies and their wives with breezy-looking blouses and fancy necklaces, one of pearl and the other of filigreed gold. They were identified as Mr. and Mrs. Earl Hansen and Mr. and Mrs. Wyatt Belsberger!

That last name ran a cold shiver through me as I scrutinized the photo. He was the fellow, all right, the white guy at the ballpark with Tom Baird! The one who'd made

Jimmy feel uncomfortable. The one who stared at me with sad, desperate eyes! He couldn't hide those unhappy eyes from the newsman's lens, even though he smiled his crooked smile. Damn, but I knew him. So that there'd be no doubt, I helped myself to the center section, to match the faces if I saw the man in public again. Aunt Monique would forgive me, as she'd probably already read the paper that morning. Now, however, I realized how serious the matter was: I'd put Jamesetta in danger by sending her on a mission that Bumpy Johnson and his stooge Leon the Spiker had warned me away from. I promised myself that if I lived through this, I'd take Aunt Monique and Jamesetta to a swell dinner and a show at the Apollo: not only for all the trouble they'd taken, and for the middle section of "The Daily News" that I'd taken, but also for the pair of crutches Monique had brought from the hotel, which I borrowed from the hall closet: They hung on a hook there in the company of a chambermaid's lost-and-found keepings. But I couldn't wait for the little lady to return that evening. I had to catch up with Jamesetta.

After binding my left foot with a rag that I found under the kitchen sink, I managed to fit my shoe on without tying the laces. I wrote Aunt Monique a note expressing my gratitude and my hope to see her soon. Then I hit the pavement, clumsily and gingerly tripping along to the subway, tilting along, really, on the crutches and my good right foot while barely touching my left toe to the cement. This wasn't an easy way to get through life. People brush past you without excuse, cars beep at you for moving too slow, and even the lame and the blind show no respect--as I discovered when a fat lady with a cane whacked me as I nearly tipped off-balance into her and when a blind man at the corner muttered an unflattering word as I told him I couldn't guide him across the street! Imagine getting through life like this, I considered, limping along from childhood to old age on a pair of stolen crutches and being cursed for your infirmity!

Worse trouble appeared on the ferry. I hobbled through the Liberty Street terminal, entered the ferry, climbed the stairs, and sat down, only to catch sight of Leon the Spiker as the boat pulled slowly out of the slip. I froze. Had Bumpy Johnson been watching me and then divining my motives in returning to Jersey City? Or was Leon simply set on by Wyatt Belsberger and Tom Baird to cut me and let me bleed? Or some combination of those two possibilities? The boat gave a heave: It was too late to get off; moreover, I supposed the thug would avoid violence among so many passengers, since he'd have no place to run while the ferry chugged its ten minutes across the Hudson. With a nod of recognition, Leon the Spiker, in slacks and sports jacket, sat across from me in the cabin, his head to one side, the wide brim on his gray fedora turned down over a sleepy-eyed stare. Glancing at my bad foot, I considered who might have sent him and how I could escape once the ferry docked. He was one meaning-looking, ugly critter, as the cowboys would say. His cheek had a lump in it, and his nose twisted to one side, maybe because I had broken it. His snarl revealed a gold tooth. He smirked and tapped his ribs occasionally, suggesting that under his two-toned sports jacket he carried a pistol or a shiv.

"Say hello to Tom Baird," I shot at him. Leon jerked his head; he seemed curious; and that told me that Baird was out of the picture. Either Bumpy or Wyatt had hired the Spiker. And why would Bumpy? He'd already dealt with me. No, the culprit, I decided, was Wyatt; and soon I'd discover I was right. (Bumpy, as it turned out, had simply referred the thug to Wyatt, for a fee.)

With that settled, I stood up quickly as the ferry entered the slip in Jersey City and started for the gate at the bow. I decided I'd make a dash for the cab stand, sprained ankle be damned. I'd put Leon and a small crowd behind me and get myself a twenty-foot head start.

I stood at the metal gate as if I were ready to run the one hundred. When the crewmen drew it back, I lunged forward. But, damn, suddenly I snagged: The rubber tip of my crutch caught a hole in the ferry's deck! The passengers shifted around me and out onto the ramp. Still working the crutch loose, I saw Leon coming for me, staring dead on. The glint of his shiv hit my eye as he held it next to his thigh. Just as he neared for the plunge, though, my crutch slipped free. It swung up and into Leon's groin. I'd already screamed for help. Some crewmen must've seen the knife as well--the passengers had all disembarked--and two came running towards us. I poked a crutch at my assailant, holding him at bay with short, quick jabs. He must've flung the knife overboard when the crewmen grabbed him and slammed him down on the deck. I no longer saw it in his hand. Just my luck, I thought: He wouldn't be arrested for a little scuffle. Still, he lay there disabled; so I hopped off, dropping a crutch, the one that nearly got me killed, as I entered the terminal.

I took a train into town, where I stopped at Toby's house, hoping to find someone at home. Hannah Hughes invited me in, asking me to stay for supper, since it was now six o'clock and they'd already sat down to eat.

"Moonbeam who?" I heard Toby's voice ring from the kitchen. Leaving my crutch in the entranceway, I followed his wife to the kitchen table and limped to a chair opposite Toby. He glared as I sat. "Hadn't you gotten the news?" he demanded. "You are no longer on the team."

"I heard."

"Then why do I have to look at you when I eat?" he muttered.

I told him why. I described my assailant, Leon the Spiker, and how he attempted to bring me down. Down to the grave. I mentioned the language he used about keeping my nose clean: exactly the words that Toby had used some days earlier. Then I described my encounter with Bumpy Johnson, the Hades of Harlem. Then I asked Toby what he knew about the three Bs: Baird, Belsberger, and Bumpy.

Toby didn't answer but continued to eat.

Hannah's pork chops smelled delicious, yet I made one objection to sharing the meal: I could handle anything but those sweet-smelling chops. If I chewed on my right side, I could manage the peas and mashed potatoes, and that was all. Such was my tribulation that warm August evening.

The meal done, Toby's silence ended. He laid down his knife and fork.

"You are a fool," he commented, "who doesn't understand the pattern." I didn't answer. "The pattern holds everything in place. Those three bases and home plate, they make a pattern we call the diamond. Now, if we went and changed the shape of that diamond every day, there'd be no way to play two games in a row, much less a whole season. There'd be no way to form teams, assign positions, organize itineraries, or contract ourselves into black, white, major, or any other kind of league. We wouldn't even have a pick-up game in a sandlot. Without a pattern, there'd be nothing."

I said I could see that.

"Then why are you trying to break the pattern?" he asked. "You know what I mean. You've been to college, so you say. I'm sure you studied a bit of philosophy, how everything exists in its own time and place. And there's no way to change that, because that's the way it is. You try to change that, and you create a mess: Chaos is what you create, for yourself and others. Take my advice and give this some thought. Don't be a fool, nigger. You'll live longer."

There was raspberry jello for dessert. It was cool and soothing in my mouth. I thanked Hannah for inviting me. Then I turned on Toby with an accusation, asking why he became part of the pattern that tried to destroy me for investigating the death of Buster Fenton.

"You're wrong on that," he said. "Those three Bs are not part of any pattern I know." He looked me straight in the eye, and I believed him. When he told me to keep my nose clean, Toby'd used tough-guy language as a manner of speaking and, as I finally saw, coincidentally with Leon. He didn't run with the wolves. Toby would always be Toby, safe in his office in the clubhouse, taking and making bets, and then coming home to Hannah for pork chops, mashed potatoes, and peas. Though he talked tough, he led a fairly decent life, inside the pattern. As for me, well, I'd made a decision, come life or death, to let the pattern be damned. It could threaten you with a shiv in the middle of the Hudson River, and it could trap you in some spooky chess game in the heart of hell. Keep you there, too. I guess my life was made for a larger and riskier reach. So I smiled a funny smile and asked him for a favor.

"I need you to contact Hank Thompson for me. Find out if Jamesetta Kelly is with him." I explained about Jamesetta and Buster; then I explained how she and I were connected. "I need to know she's safe." I reminded him that Thompson was the young second baseman for the Monarchs, who were still in town. ("I know who Thompson is," Toby growled.) "Well, he may be at The Huntsman's Bar and Grille with the other players." I explained that Thompson was Baird's chauffeur at times as well as his prize infielder. I also mentioned that he had a chance to break the pattern by signing with the New York Giants but that Baird sensed this and kept him close and paid him extra. I also mentioned that Thompson accompanied Baird to Harlem for Buster's last dinner.

"You don't say," said Toby.

"I do."

"I don't know," he hesitated. "Why can't you listen to me?"

"I will, Toby, I will. Give me till next week." I smiled, a simple, humble smile, not too broad, since my jaw had begun to ache again, even after I'd avoided the pork chops, good as they smelled. "Just call the saloon and ask for him. Tell him you have a man here representing the president of a Major League baseball team."

He turned to Hannah, who silently pleaded my case.

"I want ten dollars out of your next pay envelope," he said, rising and going for the telephone.

"One thing more," I nodded, agreeing. "Ask him to bring along Miss Jamesetta Kelly, if she happens to be there. By now I'd hoped she'd be speaking to him."

"She was Buster's fiancée, you said?"

"I did."

Toby shook his head, dialing.

Within fifteen minutes Thompson showed up, alone. Grabbing my crutch, I drew him outside the house, where we got into his green 2-door Chevy coupe, which he rode with the rumble seat open, and drove to a desolate section of town, parking near a factory on an empty street. Hank wanted to know why Mr. Stoneham hadn't contacted him directly. Then he wanted to know what the devil I had to do with these negotiations. I embroidered a tale as best I could, explaining that the Giant owner had a fear of Tom Baird's spies, meaning his scouts, which he imagined went everywhere you found a baseball game. By coincidence, I went on, I happened to be in Mr. Stoneham's office that very morning. So he enlisted me to get to him, Hank Thompson, best rookie slugger in the Negro League. In fact, I said, Stoneham had seen Thompson's home run on Sunday, and now he was sure he wanted him for the big leagues. Everyone knew that Horace Stoneham was ga-ga over the power hitters, among whom he thought Thompson the most promising.

"He expects to see you tomorrow in his office. It's inside the clubhouse in deep centerfield in the Polo Grounds." All this contained a vague sort of truth. I'd judged the Giant owner as hoping for Thompson to drop by last week, when the Monarchs came to town. Hadn't I gained entrance when I introduced myself as him? All Hank would have to do is use his rightful name. Didn't Stoneham want his own Jackie Robinson? Hadn't he already, in some way, led Thompson on? Moreover, I'd noticed him standing and clapping in the box seats at Roosevelt Stadium yesterday for that 400-foot blast slammed by the young man sitting next to me in the Chevy coupe--Baird's Chevy coupe. Stoneham just didn't know how to get around that--that grip that Baird had on Hank.

This hopeful Major League slugger had an open, square face. He blended into a crowd easily, but once you singled him out, you wouldn't be encouraged to go over and start a conversation. In spite of his outward calm, he had a subtle edginess. Not a man with many friends, he had the reputation of being a brooder. Like Boondocks Cooney, it wasn't hard to get him into a fight. It was known that he carried a gun. And now his face assumed a curious tension as he tightened his mouth, squinting at me, trying to see how far he could trust me, how much he'd owe me for the favor.

"You work for Tom Baird," I went to my main point. "I mean, off the field as well as on. I heard you were at that dinner with Buster and his girl at Helen's."

He nodded tentatively.

"You remember Jamesetta Kelly there, right?" He nodded. "Well, then, have you seen her today? I sent her ahead to seek you out. For the good news."

He denied seeing her.

"I needed her to go on ahead of me because of my injury," I continued. "Some fellows gave me a hard time last night."

He stared blankly.

"Turns out baseball's a dangerous game," I added. No reaction.

"Was that Wyatt Belsberger who substituted that spiker for Leon Latortue in the game last week?"

He nodded slowly, yes.

With that settled, I returned to Jamesetta.

"Okay. That night at Helen's. You sat with Baird, Buster, and her. Then Buster went out and got himself killed." Another tight-faced look.

"Buster got killed because of a white woman." His head jerked up. "How'd you know that?"

Well, now, that was a point squarely settled.

"Word gets around," I replied. "Matter of fact, I heard it from Horace Stoneham."

I could see that Thompson was impressed. On the force of this reaction, I decided to appeal to Hank's youth, his human side, and his racial loyalty.

"That night the man died," I said, "after he dropped off his fiancée, and that was after he left you and Mr. Baird at the restaurant, right?" No word back.

"He died because he was young and black and talented, not much different from you, Hank. I'd say he died partly because he wanted to move up in the white man's league and partly because he wanted to take the white man's woman."

145

Thompson turned away, his eyes fixed, it seemed, on the fire hydrant across the street.

"But maybe I got some of the details wrong. Maybe Buster left his girlfriend at the door and then went and picked up this white babe. Maybe you drove him to do just that," I started guessing.

"Who told you that?" He kept his eyes averted.

Bingo.

"Tom, Tom Baird told me that. He told me to get the whole story from you." This was at least half true.

"He did?"

"Yeah, you know him. He couldn't tell me everything. But I can tell you this: If anything goes haywire, Horace Stoneham has promised me to cover you. You'll be protected. He has definite plans for you."

I reached into my pocket and gave him Stoneham's five-dollar bill.

He held the bill between thumb and fingers, rubbing it. He regarded me as suddenly having a third dimension--or even a fourth. He gave a snorting sort of laugh. He took a quick, suspicious glance back at me, as if I had some supernatural connection with the white world. Suavely, with a smooth gesture, he stuffed the five-dollar bill into his shirt pocket. Then he shrugged, lit a cigarette, and told me the story.

It wasn't too complicated, and it was fresh in his memory.

After taking Jamesetta back to her aunt's, Buster'd returned to Helen's on 110th Street, where he found Barbara waiting for him in a cab. He invited her into Helen's for a drink, believing that everyone had left. But Hank had lingered at the bar: He was killing an hour or so as Baird was off somewhere at another meeting in midtown. He'd have to pick him up there later. Buster had already dismissed the cab; so they asked Hank to drive them to Brooklyn, where Barbara stayed at the Hotel St. George. They'd give Hank ten bucks. They were in great spirits, talking about how Buster would come to her hotel room dressed as a bellboy, and so spend the night. What a picture. They laughed as Hank drove, the two lovers sitting up front with the driver.

Once over the Manhattan Bridge, Hank mentioned they were on Flatbush Avenue, not ten minutes from Ebbets Field, where Jackie Robinson would soon play ball. Both Buster and Barbara got excited at the prospect of seeing the home field of the Brooklyn Dodgers. Agreeably, Hank drove up Flatbush Avenue, since he too had gotten excited about the idea. He asked for directions around Prospect Park and then found the ballpark. Under the yellow moonlight, they saw the big letters EBBETS FIELD over the entranceway. They asked Hank to stop and get out with them since nothing but walking around the stadium would satisfy them. But it was twelve-thirty in the morning, and Hank had to be back in Manhattan to pick up Baird at one. Moreover, he'd been spooked by their talking so freely about their love affair, especially with the image of Buster as a bellboy: so he insisted on leaving. They offered him a few more dollars, which he refused. So they told him to go back to Mr. Baird and keep quiet about the drive. Then they got out of the car, telling him they'd catch a cab to the St. George.

He stopped talking to light another cigarette with the first one.

He told me he left them on the vacant corner of Sullivan Place at the main entrance of Ebbets Field. He returned, then, to pick up his boss in Manhattan, driving him back home to Jersey City through the Holland Tunnel.

When I asked him if Buster had signed a contract to play for KC, Hank shook his head, saying, "He wanted a day to think about it."

A day that never came.

"You shoot him?" I asked point blank.

He looked surprised.

"I mean, you never know: He was competition."

"You're hearing it like it was," he asserted, eyes straight at me.

I believed him. There was more than one team after him. Why would he mess up his chances?

"What about Wyatt Belsberger?" I asked. "Crazy sonofabitch or what?"

He hesitated.

"I know he came to New York with Baird," I said. "What the hell was he doing here?"

Hank claimed he didn't clearly know. Aside from his financial interest in the Monarchs, Wyatt was an old buddy of Baird's. They'd played some baseball together once, even though Baird had been some years older than Wyatt. They laughed at a lot of jokes Hank could never figure out. Hank saw Wyatt show Baird that he carried a pistol. Was that pistol meant to be used on Buster? Didn't Hank know that Barbara was Wyatt's wife?

"Yeah, man, sure. But what the hell. How was that my business?" he said. "I thought she was a pretty nice lady." He smiled. He'd made ten bucks from her.

"Yeah, but . . . ."

"But nothing. Buster didn't die from gunshot, did he?"

"No, but . . . ." I stopped. He didn't want to hear about Wyatt's guilt. Too close to home, I supposed. "Nothing like keeping cool," I said.

What about the next day, I wondered. How did Baird discover that Buster'd been killed? The answer was obvious. When Buster didn't phone the next day, Baird got anxious. Hank suggested he contact the Hotel St. George and ask for Miss Iris Hampton, which was Barbara's made-up name. That's when both he and Baird learned there'd been a horrible mess earlier that morning.

So Hank drove his boss over to Brooklyn. At the hotel they were surprised to find Wyatt and Barbara Belsberger in the lobby, surrounded by policemen. As the cops questioned Barbara, Wyatt slipped from the encirclement to speak anxiously to Baird. Thompson wasn't part of the conversation since the two men went over to the telephone stations and spoke out of hearing, with Wyatt frantic and gesturing wildly. Hank could see them from the lobby. Then both men nodded, shook hands, and came back to the police. Hank's assessment was that Baird would use his influence to work something out for his desperate friend.

With an alibi?

Possibly.

Thompson seemed to have mixed feelings about his boss's apparent collusion in a cover-up; but since this left him off the hook--after all, he'd chauffeured the giddy lovers to Brooklyn--he didn't bother to think further about it. Of course, he had no deep feelings for Buster, whose death left him at the head of the field; and yet he'd felt regret because he could understand Buster's situation: he'd had a white girlfriend himself once: and on the sneak, too. Moreover, Buster and he were the same age, had hit equally well that summer, had played footsie with Horace Stoneham while, on the other hand, dealing with Tom Baird, and each one saw himself as the next Negro athlete in the Major Leagues. Hank was mostly agreeable to me, who he didn't see as competition; yet I sensed a confused soul in him. He entertained a mass of contradictions behind his square-faced placidity; he carried a gun, as I said, and could be easily provoked in a saloon after a few drinks.

So far he hadn't drunk much today. He'd just gotten to The Huntsman when Toby called there. In my pose, I remained undisturbed by his revelations, shaking my head and smiling easily as they came to the surface. Once Thompson's tale was done, I asked for one more favor, a ride over to the Liberty Street Ferry.

"Tell me," he insisted; "what is your business in all this?"

"I'm an undercover detective," I replied. He reacted, but I clapped his shoulder and added: "Unofficial, man." He could make of that what he wanted. It was no lie.

"Unofficial?" he echoed.

"Yes." I winked. "I'll never use your name in this investigation," I promised. "But, remember, this is murder we're talking about."

Somehow it dawned on him that I'd gotten him to talk more than he should have. He shifted suspiciously. Who knows what connection I had with the white man? He knew the limits of his connection with Baird, but he had no idea of my larger identity. Still, this was a serious turn, now that he spilled the beans on himself and his boss. And Wyatt. And Barbara too.

Imagination is a tricky thing. He felt himself around his chest and waist, making sure his pistol was within ready grasp. Then I touched his wrist.

"Hank," I assured him, "it's cool. You're cool, man. You won't be implicated. Trust me."

Of course, he had to. Trust me or shoot me.

Then I mentioned again the protection he'd get from Mr. Stoneham.

Breathing deeply, he started the engine, looking straight ahead. As darkness had fallen, he put on his headlights. Then he drove me over to the ferry without a word.

"One thing more, Hank," I said as we reached the ferry. He sighed, but I had to risk asking this: "I need your rod. They wouldn't give me one": implying that my unofficial rank in the Police Department had racial overtones. "If I run into trouble with Wyatt or his thugs, I want a fighting chance." He stared, more astonished than angry. "Seriously, Hank," I went on, "I'll get myself killed otherwise. I need protection."

He shook his head slowly. A smirk formed on his lips. He spit out the car window.

"You don't know how much I have to fight against," I continued. "Here's Buster dead, and a black man doesn't have the right to a decent police investigation. Think about that, Hank. The kid was no stumblebum; he was a hero. And they let him get murdered; and they try to stop me everywhere I turn. A man's got to have fighting chance."

He was thinking.

So I added: "The last thing you need is to get pulled over in this roadster, get slapped down, and then get thrown in the clink for carrying an unlicensed pistol."

He sneered and tossed a disgusted, backhanded wave at me. That was the least of his worries. We weren't in New

York City, where they had a Sullivan Law. This was New Jersey, where Mr. Baird told him it would be all right.

His bravado seemed to give him a touch of confidence--or was it fear? I mean, there were gun laws here, too, but who knew what they were? With a heavy, dark-eyed glance from under his eyelids, he inhaled and exhaled slowly. Then he removed a black leather hip holster with its little silver pistol snapped into it. He handed it all to me.

"Thanks, man," I said. "You're real handsome. For one thing, you gonna be square with Mr. Stoneham. I know some things. You gonna be in the Major Leagues. That's no bull. I'll give this piece back to you when I see you next. At the game. If I lose it, I'll give you the money for a new one. If I'm still alive."

CHAPTER TEN

"Glove's Great Moment"

I wasn't afraid of Hank Thompson, because if he were a killer or even only a stooge, he's the one Wyatt would've used to spike me. Moreover, the Monarchs' chief executive had better expectations for him, either as a player for KC or in a deal with the Majors. So Baird kept him close as a chauffeur and a bodyguard. That, however, didn't make him less fearsome to look upon, though Thompson's agreeable attitude confirmed his boss's innocence. There in the green Chevy was another chance to get at me, and Thompson was, instead, pretty decent.

By this time Jamesetta, without having found Hank, would be heading back to Harlem. I fretted, therefore, that she courted trouble by being out and around in New York and not back in Philadelphia where she'd avoid interest, what with Belsberger and his alluring wife still in town and Leon the Spiker on the loose, supplied with a new weapon.

And those Belsbergers. It certainly seemed as if they were trying to slip out of the country. I wondered if they headed back to KC for the next six weeks before returning to travel to England on the Queen Elizabeth; or maybe visited her folks in Philadelphia. As for their staying in the Hotel St. George, that was out, given Buster's demise. Therefore, if they were still in New York, they'd probably be at the Waldorf Astoria or some such nice midtown hotel. My object was to isolate Barbara to hear the rest of the Ebbets Field story and then, if she were innocent, to bring her husband to justice.

First, however, I wanted to be sure that Jamesetta was home again with her aunt.

Wallking onto the ferry, I noticed that the second crutch stood propped against the side of a green-slatted utility building between the terminal and the dock--waiting for me; yes, the exact one I dropped escaping from that broken-nosed Leon. I guess no one needed an extra crutch that Monday afternoon; while someone, expecting its user to make a return trip, set it there for the invalid's return. How things can be so easy.

The ferry ride across the Hudson was smooth and serene.

Nine-thirty p. m., and the moon was down. The summer night had a clear dark-blue tint of starlight above the towering silhouettes of the distant skyline. During the ten-minute passage, I set my eyes on the countless stars, feeling the boat move forward with its push-and-rock rhythm against the south-flowing river. Casually I glanced at the crutches I'd placed against the railing. They looked detached, isolated, objects with a purpose once and then, perhaps, without purpose forever, just there; to be hung up as storage in a widow's closet. Breathing the fresh air tossed against my face, I rested my forearms on the cool metal railing, my head turned upward. Eyes again on the stars, I questioned my own purpose, my own life, me, this speck of breathing, dark-skinned dust, riding in flow motion across this mindless river, flowing out of a big continent in a bigger world that was itself a mere speck in the universe's mysterious, enormous space. Insignificant as I was, I felt alive, strong, purposeful as I never had, even if in exercising my flow against all the evil currents in their counter-crosses I might bring myself to death. So I questioned: Did I have a use, was I serving a purpose, and, if so, what matter in this great sea of to-and-fro motion, all this jostling and running about, all this tripping over my own feet and everyone else's? Once done, would I be set aside like those crutches, waiting in eternity for what, nothing--or another occasion to be of use?

There was no moon, but I had a moonbeam in my pocket. So I told myself, believing that in whatever motion a man travels, he carries his own darkness and his own light. Hopefully, my light would lead me somewhere among the stars.

The ferry went bumpity-bump into the slip, causing the wooden piles to squeak as if in pain, leaning away from the boat and then easing back again. The water sloshed in white foam beneath. Seagulls rose into the dock lights and off into the night, squawking with their raspy, one-note bird-voices. As the ferry came to rest against the ramp, I moved forward with the other passengers. Soon we all disembarked onto Manhattan streets, my reverie done and the impetus to solve one crime and prevent any other sending me outward.

When I reached Aunt Monique's, the little lady had me come inside, signaling for me to enter, as if we conspired together. She explained that her niece had returned at seven that evening but stayed only a few minutes before leaving again when a white lady, a peroxide blonde, stopped by in a car to pick her up. She'd tried to stop her from going, but Jamesetta assured her that she'd be all right.

"Too bad, too bad," said her aunt, wringing her hands.

"To go where?"

She didn't know.

A peroxide blonde: evidently, Barbara Belsberger. But how and why Jamesetta?

"I see you borrowed my crutches," said Aunt Monique, glad to have them back. She kept her apartment like a museum of lost articles, supposing they'd all be useful someday to somebody--and then returned. "Did they help?"

I said they did; I said they were the biggest help I'd had in a week.

Right now I wanted to wash up and rest a while. My shirt was soggy with perspiration, wrinkled, and somehow soiled with ferry grease. When I excused myself to use the bathroom, Monique encouraged me to take a bath and leave my clothes in the hamper. She'd have underwear, shirt, and socks ready for me when I was done. Apparently, Uncle Wiley was near my size, for as I soaked in the tub Monique stealthily placed these articles inside the bathroom door. They fit nicely. After I dropped my own clothes into the hamper, she knocked gently and, when I opened the door, handed me another article, saying, "Try these too." They were Uncle Wiley's trousers, a pair of baby-blue pegged pants with dark blue pistol pockets on the backside and double saddle stitching along the outside seam revealing a dark blue stripe from front pocket to cuff. These fit nicely too. Ah, yes, that Wiley Maynard had been one cool cat.

A pair of black pointy-toed shoes waited for me in the parlor. The left shoe fit tightly over my still-swollen foot but felt good for that reason. The right shoe was loose; so I slid into my own brown wing-tipped shoe, telling myself that nobody would see the difference at night. The little lady had Wiley's sky-blue, knee-length zoot suit jacket with dark blue velvet lapels and large side pockets, but I declined to wear it, begging the heat. On a shelf in her armoire, I'd seen a low-crowned, wide-brimmed brown felt hat with a little yellow feather and perhaps, I imagined, a ten-foot-long gold watch chain too! If Wiley only knew what happened to his custom-made clothes; or, vice-versa, if they knew what happened to him! I didn't ask to see if these items might fit, since I didn't mean to disguise myself in a total transformation of dress. A lot of flash was not my style.

About to leave again, I started for the door when Monique scurried after me, begging me to sit down at the kitchen table. She'd made some tea and sandwiches, insisting I fortify myself with nutrition before I ventured off into unknown places.

"Where will you go?" she asked.

I hesitated, then shrugged. I didn't exactly know. The point was to keep moving. Perhaps I'd start at the Waldorf and ask for Barbara the peroxide blonde or maybe Wyatt the jealous maniac. Fatigue, however, began to cloud my brain. I'd had too much of a hot bath. I stood there, dithering. Suppose I ran into Bumpy's goons along the way? On the other hand, suppose Jamesetta had been kidnapped by Mrs. Belsberger and lay tied up in the trunk of a car? Then, again, suppose it was all much ado about nothing and Jimmy had merely gone off to have a bite to eat and a little talk with Barbara B.? Suppose she was about to return to Aunt Monique's?

I breathed an easy sigh. Since I hadn't eaten much at Toby's, I agreed to have supper with the sympathetic, sweet-voiced lady, this petite creature with the timid eyes and busy hands that needed to help.

"It's the most sensible thing to do now," she advised.

I agreed. I went and sat at the kitchen table and nibbled at the spiced ham sandwiches--on white bread divided into squares with the crusts sliced off. I sipped the tea. What did a gangster like Wiley Maynard want with a woman like this, I wondered. By the same token, what did she want with him? His first name should have made her suspicious. And so the more I nibbled and sipped, the tireder I grew and the more gallant. Aunt Monique suddenly looked charming to me, like a pretty mouse with her blue eyes and pert, pointy nose, and prim lips. I told her what a treat it was to be sitting and eating with her. I thanked her solemnly with a short bow. I said that if I ever got married again I'd choose a woman like her. Then I set my teacup down and wiped my mouth with a linen napkin. I rose and walked to the front door. On the way through the hall, I glanced at the couch in the parlor to see if I hadn't forgotten anything. Then I walked in and sat on it; and as I did, I leaned and lay full-length on the cushions with my feet dangling over the edge. I fixed a throw pillow under my head and drifted off into a gentle sleep.

As I did, I recall Monique saying, "Well, maybe not me. Maybe one of the family. Maybe Jamesetta."

I woke up at eight o'clock the next morning! I'd slept in the parlor for almost seven hours and came to consciousness only as Aunt Monique summoned me.

"Too bad, too bad," she intoned over me. "Now, wash up and then come and have breakfast," she uttered as I opened my eyes. She turned and went into the kitchen. I could hear bacon crackling on the stove. I smelled it too, along with fresh-perked coffee and eggs fried in butter. I couldn't believe I'd slept so long. I felt that Monique should not have let me, knowing the urgency in keeping her niece from danger. A little too much into the hostessing routine, I thought, rousing myself quickly and preparing for the day. Still, where would I be without a decent breakfast and the information that would go with it?

I'd needed the rest. Today I felt strong and clear. My left foot no longer swelled, and I could walk without crutches. The pain had gone. As I exercised my foot, I realized that

Monique had removed my shoes, the brown one and pointy black one, and eased my stockinged feet onto the couch to give me a good night's rest. I realized, too, that she'd saved me-- once she'd heard the message from the druggist, who by chance had opened the store at nine p.m. for an emergency prescription--from a horrible night of hopping around town on a wild goose chase, wearing two differently-colored shoes and Uncle Wiley's fancy blue pegged pants. This morning I could go back to wearing my own clothes and continue my quest for justice.

The little lady walked outside with me, allowing me to descend the stoop by two steps before she planted a kiss on my forehead and handed me the centerfold from yesterday's "Daily News" that she'd salvaged from my clothes when I bathed. Even though she mumbled, "Too bad, too bad," I knew she meant that kiss to mean that she trusted me as a man who'd never harm a lady, least of all her delicate, vulnerable, and adventuresome niece. I said thank you and went off to Roosevelt Stadium, where Jimmy and Barbara, according to the druggist's message, would meet me at the entrance.

Barbara was biggish, blue-eyed, and blonde, about fifteen years older than Buster. Seeing her look around from a distance, I expected her to scream when I approached, hand extended, but she only smiled, said hello, and went back to looking dazed and sorrowful. Although she seemed something of a rich, spoiled floozy who'd taken advantage of a young athlete, I couldn't hate her as I expected I would. She was glamorous in her way, and in some ways just my type, but there was something about her that warned me off, even though I hasten to admit that half the Bluebirds in the dugout would've given their eyeteeth to have a chance at her. I found her more than a tad fleshy, though probably she'd been prettier and shapelier when younger. Still, she was attractive. I saw what Buster had seen in her. She had a full bosom, revealed in her white blouse's neckline, cool for summer wear. She was attractive. Her skirt was blue and her straw hat was red--the ensemble having a patriotic appearance--with a black band. As we shook hands, I saw she wore black gloves: her colors now giving the impression of slight derangement, like those of someone who'd wandered into a strange dream. Her manner was pleasant, although her pale blue eyes had that teary look you associate with a drinker. It was those eyes that told me to be careful, yet for some reason I couldn't help but feel sympathy for her. I sensed she was a lonely one. Once introduced to her, I took out the newspaper centerfold, checking it for a match: There she was, and there was Wyatt too. When I showed it to her, she asked to keep it.

"You think this resembles me?" she asked.

I said it was a fair copy. She smiled.

Next to her, Jamesetta appeared pert, not so glamorous, but by now I saw her distinctively plain beauty, if I could describe it as such; and I wondered how Buster could've traded her for the other. But, as the Frenchman says, everyone has his own tastes, or what one man adores, another man may find just so-so. How can you argue about that?

We had an hour before the game started, and so we walked around the ballpark, talking. They talked; I listened. It was quite a story, which you will hear soon.

As we walked into the stands, I asked the more immediate question: What were these two doing together? How did they find each other? Where did they go last night?

They answered, each in her turn. Mrs. Belsberger had heard about Jamesetta from Buster, who confided to her that he and his fiancée were planning to marry next summer and were considering a contract with either The New York Giants or the KC Monarchs. After Buster's death, she'd tried phoning his parents, with no luck. Then she tried phoning the Kellys in Philadelphia, but how many Kellys could she call? That's when she remembered Jamesetta's Manhattan connection. She discovered the girl's whereabouts from the registry of the Abyssinian Baptist Church--that being the one church she'd heard about in Harlem. The white woman simply had to ask the church secretary about the girl who dated the up-and-coming black baseball player: It was no problem, glad to please. Directed now to Aunt Monique's, she found Jimmy there--and yesterday persuaded the girl to drive with her to Philadelphia to show her Buster's grave.

Oh, yes, Barbara'd gotten a car of her own, the '46 gray Packard, rented for week from a dealer in Manhattan. There it was parked, on the street right alongside Roosevelt Stadium.

Normally, Jamesetta would've been wary of a white woman popping up in a big car and asking for her at her aunt's; but this Barbara appeared so open and sincere--and so obviously unhappy--that Jamesetta decided to give her a chance. Of course, curiosity had a lot to do with it. The adventure had begun: so why not follow through on this sudden surfacing of the peroxide blonde? It was a good move, I hasten to add. For though you might anticipate some sort of animosity between the two women, there developed, instead, a kind of mutual appreciation. They'd lost the same man, and women are strange when it comes to death. Meanwhile, along the way to Philadelphia, Barbara told Jimmy quite a lot.

I had seats for the ladies behind our dugout along the first base line. The two provided a distraction for the players, who kept twisting their heads to gawk at the pair of lovelies so oddly matched. Naturally, word got out that they were both involved with Buster Fenton; so that Buster's belated reputation as a Casanova kept his fame alive among a few Bluebirds for while thereafter. Yet for others his shadow had already passed from the earth. In only two weeks. "Buster? Buster who?" I heard some teammate ask. I think it was the new guy, John Ellis, and he was serious.

Ordinarily an interesting spot, third base was as dull as the Gobi Desert that afternoon and just as hot. I stood in the coach's box, since that was where Toby decided to put me in my condition: my only action, wiping and wiping the sweat off my brow. It hardly mattered whether the wiping was a signal or not, since both pitchers were unhittable, and no man on either team reached base, not against Boondocks Cooney, for us, or Satchel Paige, for them. Not until the top of the eighth inning when Hank Thompson, playing second base for the

Monarchs, slapped the ball over the fence to make the score 1-0.

Satchel got cocky in the bottom of the inning, thinking we were sunk and he'd pitch a no-hitter. He walked Herman Glove, the first batter. Then he struck out Cooney on three pitches, swinging; this, in spite of Franklin Byrd's sign for him to take; only, Boondocks had no memory for signs. But Satchel was playing tricks, I could see, tempting Glove to steal second base by going into a slow, spidery wind-up, all arms and legs, and then throwing nearly wild to his catcher, the huge Jesse Rogers. Of course, he didn't expect Glove to attempt a steal: He was trying to make Herman feel slow by hesitating to run against him, even when everyone else in the league would have gone. And Glove wasn't leading more than two small steps off first base. Herman must've been the slowest man in big-time baseball. He also knew that Paige was into his "game," super-confident as usual. To taunt Herman, Paige threw five lob-balls to his first baseman, balls so slow in their descent that an average runner could've dashed off to second base before they were caught. Well, Herman didn't dare take a lead now; and I could see Ol' Satch with a sly grin under his foxy mustache facing the next batter, my substitute, the rookie John Ellis, all of twenty years old and playing his third full game of Negro League ball.

Ellis had struck out twice already. So he was scared and embarrassed but, as I saw it, no fool. He was a college boy from Virginia, just as I'd been from Maryland, and so I'd warned him before the game about not buckling under to the great one on the mound. Whatever Satchel might do to him, I advised him to find a way to do back to Satchel. And this is what he did.

What Satchel had up his sleeve was to entertain himself at Glove's and Ellis's expense, working his way at leisure to the final outs of a no-hitter. His object, see, was to throw beautiful, chest-high meatballs to Ellis, the kind a decent batter will hit for a line-drive over the shortstop into left center for a single. The idea was to give Ellis an apparent hit but then to have the centerfielder pick up the ball on one bounce and throw the slog-footed Glove out at second: no single, then, and two men down. The last out would be easy, probably a strikeout. Satchel had to lie awake nights thinking of such things.

Now here came the KC centerfielder--the real Leon Latortue--tiptoeing in and to his right to be in perfect position for the rookie's line drive. Oh, you Satchel, I thought. Here was his victory hanging like a ripe plum on the branch; and here just a bit of fun to humiliate the conquered team. (I should add here that before the game Satchel had called me over to the Monarch's dugout and introduced me to this Leon, someone with a similar build but no facial resemblance to the Spiker. I also thanked Satchel again for his talk with me but didn't continue beyond the pleasantries. I knew he knew things but didn't want to get too far into them, and I had to respect that.) Here, now, came the first pitch, like an ice cream sundae, right across the plate, letter-high. Strike one. Ellis looked over at me for a sign. I indicated, "Swing," as what must be must be. So on the next pitch he swung. It was the exact pitch as before, as I'd expected, but Ellis couldn't touch the ball, he was so nervous and bamboozled trying to play Paige's game. Strike two. Again the rookie looked back at me. I gave him the same sign--I knew that Satchel knew my signs by now--only with a slight, undetectable difference, and that said, "Bunt." And that, on my part, was a stroke of genius.

Ellis stepped back out of the batter's box and looked again. I didn't pay him any attention; instead, I walked over and kicked third base, then stepped backwards into the coach's box. I saw the kid heave a sigh of desperation as he took his stance. Bunting with two strikes made no sense whatsoever. But he was a rookie, and he'd better obey the signs--that was my attitude. The bunt was the last move anybody'd anticipate, and that was its beauty, if it worked. If it didn't, the kid was going to be out anyway. All I had to rely on was Ellis's getting the feel of the tactic, which he did. It worked better than any of us would've imagined.

The third pitch came in as handsome as the other two: an easy one to bunt, as I'd counted on. At the last split-second

Ellis crouched and tapped the ball towards third base. The bunt was so perfect and so surprising, the stands let forth a roar. I could feel the crowd behind me rise up in pure appreciation. Satchel had no way to grab the little nubber; and by the time the third baseman got to it, Ellis was two steps from first base. Glove, however, still moved like a slow freight train halfway to second. The third baseman had him dead. Trouble was, the fielder, off-balance and angry for being caught playing deep at third, reared back and threw too high and too hard. The ball sailed over the second baseman's head into right centerfield, where nobody thought to cover. I believe I saw Glove leap when he knew the ball was loose on the outfield grass. After his foot touched second base, he came striding towards third like a man who'd sold his soul to the devil for extra speed. He was twenty years old again and chugging like a new locomotive. I signaled "up" at third and sent him on ahead. He cornered the base, lighting for home. The gleam in his eye was nothing less than demonic.

Soon the rightfielder scooped the ball off the outfield grass and threw to the cut-off man at second base; the second baseman whirled and pegged to the catcher. Herman Glove was about six feet from the plate when the ball hit the catcher's mitt. The catcher was bent over in perfect position on the third base side; so that Herman's one chance lay in a head-on collision--maybe only the threat of one--as he came full throttle towards home. But the KC catcher, like Herman, was no stripling. He was Jesse Rogers, six-foot-three and two hundred and forty pounds. He held his ground. Then the irresistible force met the immoveable object, and both players fell across the plate in a smokescreen of dust. Everyone looked for the ball, our side praying it lay on the ground near home plate, their side praying the catcher gripped it in his mitt.

The Good Lord apparently favored the Monarchs' prayers over ours, as with a gravelly voice, the umpire sang, "You're out!" dramatically swinging his right arm up, then pointing his finger to the Bluebirds' dugout.

But Herman would have no truck with that call, not after the greatest running effort of his baseball career. He rolled over, rose up, and, standing over the diminutive umpire, pushed his face down against the man's mask. As Herman unleashed a flow of invective, I stared at the other fellow in his blue shirt, noticing for the first time how short he was! He looked as if Herman would knock him over with the force of his breath.

"You crazy? You blind behind those iron bars? You sneak in here and masquerade as an umpire? You like a monkey who don't know the game, much less see it. You ain't worth two nickels they pay you to stand there and fuck up every play!" And so on and so on.

Things came more and more unloose. Satchel stood there on the mound expressionless, dumbfounded to watch his flow motion upset in chaos. Jesse Rogers, whose play had saved the day for the Monarchs, sat dazed on the plate, as if not realizing where he was. The umpire, as if scared of violence from Herman, limped several steps towards first base, as if he'd been hurt in the scramble. But then I recalled he'd been limping all afternoon. I'd paid him no attention, being occupied with my own thoughts, worrying about Wyatt Belsberger and everything else. Anyway, to avoid further embarrassment for Herman and the umpire, I jogged over to hold back our fiery red devil of a catcher, if Glove could ever be any other color but dark brown; for now he galloped around in front of the little guy and repeated his litany of abuse: "You crazy, etc., etc." Before I could reach him, however, the umpire spun away from him, whipping off his mask with a disgustful gesture and then his hat. As he did, I came face to face-- with the bald janitor of the Brooklyn apartment house on Bedford Avenue!

For five long seconds the action stopped as we both stared in wonder, trying to recall where we'd seen the other. As soon as the recognition kicked in, I took a quick look over the Bluebird dugout to find the faces of Jamesetta and Barbara, when to my horror I saw their seats were empty. Had they both gotten up to buy some peanuts and a Coke? I doubted that. I knew instantly they'd been subject to some sort of violence, that they'd been taken away by force, that they'd been kidnapped! Damn. Damn. When did that abduction take place? The game had been so lazy and then so rambunctious I'd forgotten my chief purpose in being there was not to coach baseball but to catch a killer. All I'd been doing was looking at the dirt and worrying. However, I remembered nodding to Jimmy as I came out of the dugout in the bottom of the eighth; so the abduction could only have occurred this inning. Was there a chance I could catch up to them outside the ball park?

"Glove," I shouted, "hold onto this fake umpire! He's an impostor! Have him arrested!" When Glove hesitated, thinking I only seconded his remarks in anger, I shouted again, "He's a killer! He helped kill Buster!" Which wasn't true, but it was true enough. Luckily, Herman understood me now. As soon as he moved on that bald-headed gimp, I started like a shot for the dugout.

"Where you going now?" demanded Toby.

"Got to change my shoes," I yelled, running past him. I have no memory of his facial reaction since I didn't care to notice: I had to act with all deliberate speed. First, though, I had to remove my spikes and get into real shoes. I couldn't be running clackety-clack down Jersey City streets, as I imagined, with little iron prongs stuck to my feet! Slipping on greasy black asphalt or catching myself in unsuspected holes and cracks was definitely to be avoided.

I've learned that even in dire emergencies it's smart to stop and get properly fitted out.

In my regular brown shoes but still in my Bluebird uniform--blue-gray flannel with a bluebird on the chest--I hurried out of the stadium as panic grew in me, hoping to catch the women and their kidnappers before they drove away. Outside, there were four cars, all black, at various spots down the street, motionless and empty. Beyond those, not a soul, not a dog, nothing but cement and asphalt stretching away and leaving me in open solitude. Most disturbingly, Barbara's gray '46 rented Packard was gone.

Suddenly I felt frightened, like an abandoned child; my heart filled with despair. A dark cloud passed over me. I shivered in the hot day, knowing my cause was lost. There was no way out of the maze. Dizzying maze it was, no simple puzzle or chess game. It was over. I felt my head go blank; and then like a bird flitting through the branches of a tree, the idea of running numbers for Bumpy Johnson fluttered through my brain. That was the only running I could do now. Forget about Buster's death; my career had ended. Why does a man need to go beyond himself, I questioned. Why enter the larger world? Why accept responsibility for a woman or a race of people--or even for myself? And those women, Jamesetta and Barbara, wouldn't they be all right? Even if they wouldn't, what could I do now?

Head almost wobbling from side to side, I took a deep breath. Then as I spun around to head back into the Stadium, I bumped into Herman Glove, himself in uniform and spikes, gulping down his breath, still fiery red under his natural color, and wanting to join me in the chase. My mind immediately changed. Herman changed it!

"Taxi," I shouted, "we need a taxi!"

"Goin' where?" he shouted back.

"Tunnel," I hollered, catching my breath, "The Holland Tunnel!"

He grabbed my shoulders. "Take my car," he insisted--he had a car?--and sped off down the street and around the corner to a black '38 Chrysler. I followed.

"Bought it yesterday," commented Herman. "Forty dollars."

We both hopped in, Herman turned on the ignition, and we headed for the tunnel. He may have forgotten to remove his spikes, but he didn't neglect to grab his car keys, and for this I was hugely grateful. Hell, I was grateful that he offered to help, since I'd felt eerily alone out there on the street. I promised myself that I'd let him call me Moomba all he wanted. Sourfaced as he often was, I was overjoyed to have his company. Even so, I asked him why he went out of his way to help. His answer was that he'd been feeling guilty about tipping Tom Baird off about Buster's negotiation with Horace Stoneham, so he felt he ought to do his part to capture Buster's killers: He'd intuited, out there on the field, exactly what I was running to do.

"Ump's under lock and key," he added as we zipped out of town. "He really in on that killing?"

"No," I replied, "but he helped with the cover-up."

As he concentrated on the road, speeding over fifty miles an hour on city streets, I thanked him for his support. "I thought you'd be mad at me," I said: that is, for flagging him around third base and sending him home.

"I was safe!" he shouted angrily. "Jesse tagged me with the glove, but he kept the ball in his other hand! Catcher's trick. I've used it myself!"

"This is more important," I said. "We got bigger fish to fry."

We were both worked up with emotion to do justice to Buster Fenton--and, of course, at this moment to save the ladies. Herman understood the predicament in some vague outline, since I'd indicated to him before the game that Jamesetta, who he'd met at the cemetery in Philadelphia, sat with Barbara Belsberger, "Buster's other interest," as I phrased it. Herman had wondered how the two could tolerate to sit together in peace. That's when I hinted that the two women were avoiding a third party who could prove dangerous.

Morever, when I left the Stadium, I didn't neglect to take the pistol I'd gotten from Hank Thompson. I told Herman about that too.

"Hmmm," he responded. That was all.

As we raced along, I filled him in on the events of the past week. I spoke of my talks with Horace Stoneham, Satchel Paige, Tom Baird, Bumpy Johnson, and Hank Thompson, and of Jamesetta's business with the white woman. I told him of Leon the Spiker's attack on me on the ferry. Then I went into the evidence against Wyatt Belsberger. He was the source of all our troubles, as I described him, and now we had to face him. Or I alone if Herman had second thoughts.

"But tell me," he wanted to know, "was I safe or out?"

"Safe or not," I answered, "you were super-colossal. You took that turn faster than ever I saw Cool Papa Bell. And if I lie, may I hope to die. So that we both know you deserved to be safe!"

He grinned. That, too, was his best ever, in the way of a smile.

"I'm in it for the prize money," he said, "come hell or high water!"

I could've hugged him, ugly as he was.

It's a crisis that brings out high character, and so it was with Herman Glove.

Bad character also arises in a crisis, and this was not a pleasant prospect for us as we neared the toll booths for the tunnel.

"Tell me more about that umpire," Herman asked.

"He's the apartment house janitor. They got the him to deny he ever knew of Buster Fenton. I'm guessing that umpiring job was his pay-off. He offered his services for a chance to participate in the game. That and a little money besides. Who's 'they'? Wyatt must've worked a deal through Bumpy Johnson: paid him a lot of mazuma to play dumb in that apartment house." I told him that Wyatt was a silent partner in the Monarchs' organization as well as Baird's good friend. "I'm not clear on Baird's involvement in the crime, because I see him as a straight arrow, a little loose in the fledging maybe, but that Belsberger is one mean, crooked cracker. I've just heard it all: that he and some hired thugs murdered Buster, then asked Baird to provide the police with an alibi. So once I saw that bald-headed gnome, I knew I had to act fast."

Now, I'd spent a good hour with Jamesetta and Barbara before the game, when the two women put the whole story to me, a bit scattered in the details; even so, I saw the general outline pretty clearly, although the two of them were so excited they spoke one on top of the other: Each put in her own two cents so rapidly I had to tell them to slow down and repeat the sequence of events. But there it was. At the same time Toby appeared and told me to go coach third base. But I knew now that Belsberger was our man, given the mess of information I'd gotten from the two women; and I felt in my bones that he would come for them--soon, very soon. And then me. However, once the game was underway, I believed the women would be safe sitting behind the dugout, where I could look over and see them. But then the game exploded, and that was when Belsberger and his goons took the opportunity to force the women to leave the stadium.

If he succeeded in harming them, he'd be back for me. And probably Glove, once he caught sight of him.

"We've got to keep our eye on the ball," I said to him. "Eye on the ball."

This was exciting. I was standing up in the game, and I loved the danger. So did Herman.

"Wyatt's the killer," I told him again. "He got some help from Baird. And the whole business involved a white woman--the one you saw with Jamesetta."

It was time to explain everything in full to Herman. He needed to understand as much as possible. At this point so do you. So here it is, the crux of the mystery.

Wyatt Belsberger had come East with his pal Tom Baird, supposedly to advise him on the negotiations with Buster; as a friend and business partner; and, additionally, to get himself a distribution contract for his potato chip company--"Bell's, a Tinkle of Taste in Every Chip!" (Actually, it was a flavorful potato chip, crisp but not too thin: I'd buy a big bag of Bell's every time we played in Missouri.) His real reason for the trip was to catch up to his wife and Buster--and then take care of Buster. So once in New York, he hired a private detective to follow his wife around to establish the locale of her adulterous behavior; while Baird, it seemed, his mind on business, had no clear idea that this love-triangle had formed and that, while it drove Buster away from the Giants, it would spell the end of the Monarchs' attempt to get him.

By the time of that dinner on 110th Street, Wyatt had already planned to kill Buster in Brooklyn. He knew his wife stayed there at the Hotel St. George; he knew, too, that Buster visited there, disguising himself as a bellboy. With vengeance in view, he made contacts and got help from Bumpy Johnson-- to set up that gnomish janitor in Flatbush (as it all came out later), only a fifteen-minute drive from the Hotel St. George, and then work out the gimmick of Buster's hanging himself in the apartment house basement.

As Barbara learned from her talk afterward with Wyatt, her husband and his men had picked up their direction that night from outside the restaurant and followed them in their own car. The hired detective had photographed Barbara and Buster here and there the city; he now drove Wyatt in a black Cadillac as they trailed the two lovebirds from one spot to another. It was actually a coincidence that Buster and Barbara had stopped at Ebbets Field, so close to the apartment house. But the execution plans had already been made; so Wyatt would have gotten Buster somewhere in Brooklyn that night or the next.

Thus, when Hank Thompson took the black ballplayer and white adulteress to Ebbets Field that carefree night, Wyatt Belsberger had a dark fate prepared for the young athlete. He sat in the Caddy with the detective, who carried the pipe, and another henchman (identified later as Leon the Spiker), who carried the rope. When they found the lovers in an unlighted spot along the stadium's wall, they struck.

Here is the scene, with Barbara and Buster walking around Ebbets Field shortly after midnight, when suddenly three men come out of the dark: Wyatt Belsberger and two thugs.

Wyatt cries out, "Get that black bastard!"

One of them cracks Buster over the head with a lead pipe, and while Buster staggers under the blow, the other loops a rope around his neck and starts choking him until he drops to the cement, unconscious. Then the two henchmen load him into the car and bring him to the Bedford Avenue basement, where the police are informed they should find him.

Okay. Back to Barbara. During the attack, while the two thugs were busy with Buster, Belsberger grabbed his wife in a choke hold and began haling her down the street with a knife pointed into her side. Reaching Bedford Avenue, he told to behave herself or he'd kill her then and there. He managed then to hail a cab, push her in, and have the cabbie take them to the Hotel St. George in downtown Brooklyn. She and Wyatt rode the cab back to the hotel, intending to spend the night there, since if she never returned to the hotel or was found to be missing the police might see some connection between Buster's death and the Belsberger pair.

Barbara, however, wanted only her luggage. She planned on leaving Wyatt there in whatever way she could. This, however, was wishful thinking on her part. Once in the hotel, with people in the lobby, Barbara saw a chance to phone the police. She hurried to the desk to make the call, but the desk clerk had disappeared and no one operated the switchboard at that hour. She behaved frantically, slipping away from Wyatt again--he'd grabbed her at the desk, only to release her when he saw other curious people nearby--and getting into the elevator ahead of him to ride upstairs to telephone from her room, only to discover that all calls from the rooms went through the main switchboard! So down she went, her head swirling with fear and confusion, her eyes dripping with tears--clawing through her purse to find a nickel to make a call at the public phone, only to meet Wyatt alone in the lobby, his lungs gasping for breath and his face twisted in anger. Coming quickly to her, he punched her in the jaw and knocked her unconscious. When she came to, she was back upstairs in her room with Wyatt.

Terrified as to what would happen to her, she listened to her husband contend that she could never testify against him in court and that any accusation she leveled against him would be ignored by the justice system. He insisted that she had forced him to do what he did by taking a lover and making him look ridiculous as a white man who'd lost his woman to a black man. What else was he supposed to do? Smile? He opined as how her extra-marital shenanigans with a Negro would hardly pass kindly with anyone, white or black, since she and Buster broke the racial laws of the nation! In some states she and Buster would go to jail for crossing that line!

"What did you do to him?" she demanded. "What are you going to do to me?"

He didn't answer, just sat there with a gun in his hand.

"Where is he? Wyatt, where is he?"

Still no answer.

"I have to know, Wyatt," she pleaded; "then I'll do what you say. I want to live."

Looking straight at her, speaking in a dull voice, he admitted the truth: "He's dead."

"How?"

"You saw how."

"How?"

"Lynched," he said, his expression part grin and part grimace.

"Oh, no." She wept, then asked: "Was there any blood?"

"No," said Wyatt. "That's why the cops are going to believe he's done it himself."

He told her afterwards that the body had been deposited in the basement of a nearby apartment building. It had all been worked out beforehand. Belsberger had only to telephone Bumpy and tell him the job had been done. Then the police received a phone call from one of Bumpy Johnson's associates, telling them there'd been a suicide in Flatbush. When the cops arrived, they saw Buster's body laid out in the basement with a rope around its neck. In an obscure corner some large, makeshift longshoreman's hook hung off the ceiling. A day later, according to plan, the bald-headed gnome--who all his grown life wanted to be part of big-time baseball--took away the hook and assured Bumpy Johnson that he'd chase away any curiosity-seekers by denying that anything had occurred on the property. His reward was as we saw, umpiring at the game between the Monarchs and Bluebirds. Wyatt had enough influence with Negro League procedures, as he had with the running of the Monarchs when he substituted Leon the Spiker, that he fitted the janitor in with no trouble.

Now, Belsberger had no way to accomplish this cover-up without the help of his old pal Tom Baird, President and co-owner of the Kansas City Monarchs, the most successful franchise in Negro baseball. How ironic that such a man, a consistent friend to the black athlete, a decent white guy at heart, could protect the murderer of Buster Fenton to the extent of offering tainted testimony to protect his misbegotten friend. Such, unfortunately, was the case--as with many cases in the grand field of American justice, where well-meaning people inadvertently helped the bigots keep the black man down! The best that can be said about Baird's connivance was that at first he believed his friend to be the injured party and then later began to exercise serious doubts, as evidenced by his hesitant behavior when Jimmy and I visited him in Jersey City. In the end, I should add, Baird spoke his part truthfully in a deposition that helped convict Wyatt.

There had to be a tragedy before he understood it all. At the time he believed Wyatt when Wyatt told him that the police were trying to frame him for the murder of Buster Fenton, on the grounds that he looked pretty guilty as a husband with an unfaithful wife. So Baird had made a few phone calls on his behalf. Only later did he begin to have doubts about his friend's innocence.

On the other hand, he didn't know Buster too well; and I suppose it was easy for him to imagine that Buster might've attacked Wyatt in a challenge for the big blonde. Still, he had to know that Wyatt Belsberger was an unwholesome character. Tom Baird was a Bible-reading man, as I've heard, and he should've kept in mind what St. Paul says about lewd companions.

The Apostle also says that we see through a glass darkly.

I do remember a few things from my early church-going days.

Enough of that.

I should add that Barbara agreed to go with her husband to England, where he promised to be good to her. She recalled that Wyatt had treated her pretty nicely the first few years of their marriage; that he had a real humorous side; and that he never used profane language in front of her. All the worse for him, that he followed the urging of his baser instincts.

Now neither he nor she would be going to Europe if I could help it.

Ed Eriksson

CHAPTER ELEVEN

"Darkness Rises"

There must've been a mishap in the Holland Tunnel that day, because as we waited on line for the toll booth, progress suddenly halted. No one was going anywhere, in or out of the tunnel. I reasoned, then, that Wyatt wouldn't allow himself to be stalled here, not with kidnapping victims in his car; so I told Glove to get out of line and proceed to the Lincoln Tunnel. Just as Herman wheeled around, I saw another car, a gray Packard, pull the same maneuver towards the front of the line. It was Barbara's, now driven by Wyatt.

He had the same idea. A car chase followed, not the easiest of pursuits, especially in heavy traffic along Highway 1 up through Hoboken. When we finally came to the Lincoln Tunnel, we met with the same problem: jammed traffic. At this point I lost sight of the Packard and knew immediately that Wyatt had another plan in mind. What might it be? Of course. It was the ferry at Weehawken, one that would take him over the Hudson River to the 42nd Street pier. So off we went again.

The ferries ran twenty minutes apart, and Wyatt and his men were not so many minutes ahead of us. So they had to be on this ferry. In the nick of time Herman Glove and I drove the last vehicle on. Seeing the crewmen drawing the metal gates together at the stern, we had to sound our horn to signal our coming down the ramp. After fitting the car in the last space on the starboard side, we stopped, got out, and ran down the two aisles of eighteen parked vehicles, searching for the women.

Meanwhile, the ferry lurched forward to begin its crossing.

Walking jerkily and hastily from one car to another and peering in the windows, we checked the two parallel rows of vehicles. Most of the cars were in the process of emptying, with their passengers going to the upper deck or down to the bow to gaze across the dark green water at the looming

Manhattan skyline. All but one, that is, and that was the gray '46 Packard that Barbara Belsberger had driven to Jersey City that day and parked on the street alongside the Stadium. Now there it was, the front car in the port side aisle. In it, two men were hunched down in the front seat, obviously to avoid being noticed. The driver was a white fellow I had not seen before, (but later discovered to be the detective who bashed Buster over the head with a lead pipe). The other was Leon the Spiker. I quickly checked the back seat to see a canvas tarp covering a lumpy bundle that moved when Leon turned and looked at me. Both Glove and I began knocking on the back side windows and gesturing to the two men to open up. We wanted the women, who we believed were under the canvas, to make themselves known.

Suddenly both front doors of the Packard opened and each man, the white guy and Leon the Spiker, emerged and began screaming.

"Thieves! Thieves! Thieves! Help! Help!"

This action set us back a bit, since who would expect the kidnappers to be identifying us as the criminals? They had moxie. I'll give them credit for that. So while Glove and I tried to figure what to do, the shouting brought a gang of crewmen to the Packard, and there we were: two Negroes, seen to be checking every car on deck. We were swift, aggressive, and noisy. Surely, we had wild looks in our eyes! It was impossible to hide among the crowd because we both wore blue-gray baseball uniforms and Glove's spikes went clackety-clack everywhere he walked on the metal deck! We both regarded each other as helpless, stupid, and caught: a desperate feeling, to be sure.

As the crew encircled us, I shook my head at Glove to warn him not to struggle. He didn't. The crew escorted us above to the pilot house, made us sit on the floor, and told us we were under arrest. There were six of them plus the captain. He appeared when I asked if we were arrested in New York or New Jersey. None of them seemed to know. However, to impress us with the idea of our arrest, in whatever state, the captain pulled out a holstered pistol from a drawer in the cabin and strapped it to his hips. The move was threatening, but I felt we could explain our business to this fellow, who might be able to help; since, after all, our uniforms might prove our claim to innocence. What ferry captain ever caught thieves dressed as baseball players? At first, however, this approach got us nowhere when, after having me stand to be slapped down, the man found Thompson's pistol jammed into my belt under my shirt.

Oh, man, I was way beyond myself now.

"This will get you ten years," the captain informed me as he held the gun up to show the others. His name was Murphy. The crewmen called him Murph.

"No, it won't," I claimed, sitting down again when he waved his hand for me to do so, "because I am a private investigator, hired by Mrs. Barbara Belsberger, the millionaire lady from Missouri, to keep her from being kidnapped by her husband. Her estranged husband. He's the criminal, not us."

"You've got to be kidding," said Capt. Murphy, speaking out of the side of mouth. He studied my Bluebird uniform; then he studied Glove's. "What're your names?"

"Carl," I said, "Carl Slyder. In my off-hours I play second base for the Jersey City Bluebirds"--indicating the bird on my chest--"of the Negro League, where I am known as Moonbeam Slyder, the man who stole home on Satchel Paige." I smiled my charming smile. "This here's my assistant, Herman Glove, the Bluebirds' catcher."

The seven men in the pilot house traded glances. They were curious expressions of dumbfoundedness, mockery, and disbelief. The Jersey City Bluebirds? The Negro League? Moonbeam Slyder? Herman Glove? These were names with no substance, fiction, bubbles in a black man's brain . . . alibis for bamboozlement . . . and car theft.

"What did you steal? From who? What? A satchel?" asked the captain.

"Home plate."

Capt. Murphy stared at me. I looked up at him. A man in his forties, he had the rough looks of a weathered seaman, with square-set jaw and mussed up reddish-brown wavy hair threaded with gray. He wore a blue captain's jacket with gold epaulets, a white shirt, and a dark blue tie. Not a man to be trifled with; but not one who was well-aware of the whole world of baseball, either. Breaking this impasse, one of the crewmen jerked his head and said:

"Yeah, Murph, right, Satchel Paige. He's a pitcher. Big, tall colored guy. I saw him pitch once. He struck out Babe Ruth!"

"Yeah, right, right," a few others chimed in. Ol' Satch, good for one more thing.

"Well," said the captain, still staring at me and Glove, "that's no justifiable reason for breaking into cars on my ferry! Even worse, with a loaded pistol! And crossing state lines with it!"

"As I told you," I said, my imagination burning like a high fever, then cooling me down as I breathed deeply: "I'm a private investigator. So now let me ask you one question: Did you take that gun from me in New York or New Jersey?"

"New Jersey," said a crewman, who quickly got a stern look from Capt. Murphy.

"Exactly," I went on. "New Jersey. Where there is no Sullivan Law and where, instead, I have a license as an armed guard for Roosevelt Stadium in Jersey City." (I'd promised myself no more lies; but in cases of life and death, exceptions had to be made.) Now, listen: You took that pistol from me before we crossed the middle of the river, so that firearm is now your responsibility, see, and not mine. Yours. Not mine. I will not serve ten years for carrying an unlicensed weapon, sir. Certainly not in New York."

Glove told me later he'd been so impressed by my defense before Capt. Murphy that he believed I'd make a pretty good lawyer. I'd surprised myself, too. I believed, for a moment, that I impressed the big man, as well.

"I'm the captain of this ferry," he said, nodding with a tight-toothed smile. "Don't you try and double-talk me. You're both under arrest, and that is how you'll stay until we dock. Then the city police will take you into custody." He glared at Herman, who sat miserably against the wall. "You're the smart one. You know when to keep your mouth shut."

"You are the captain, for sure," I agreed. "Indeed you are. On this ferry you are the law. We both understand that. I've recognized that from the start. We offer no trouble."

On that point the crewmen began nodding at each other; the captain, too, nodded, breathing deeper and resting his hand on the gun in his holster. I realized that the fancy talk had gotten me nowhere, except maybe to have them all pay attention to me, more than they'd pay to a true thief. So still talking, I directed their interest to the Packard and Wyatt's two henchmen.

"Please, sir," I went on, "Mr. Captain, I ask you for one thing, and that is to save two women who are held captive in the back seat of that gray Packard up front. They are tied and gagged"--as I imagined--"and hidden under a brown canvas tarp, like packages. Women carried like contraband. Please, sir, send one of these men to check. It's a question of vice, and it is crossing state lines. That's the real crime on this ferry."

Weighing this possibility, the captain rubbed his chin with two fingers. He didn't want to look stupid, being played for a sucker by two black derelicts. On the other hand, he was the captain, responsible for upholding the law governing interstate traffic. He ruminated: because, to compound the question, if he did have women on board, and in such a compromising situation, he might've needed to turn the ferry around and head back to New Jersey, criminals and state lines being what they were. By now he'd realized that he'd have to do the same with us, if we were liable to criminal indictment! He couldn't just hand us over to New York's arresting officers! Supposing I just did have a gun license? Somewhere. Life can get complicated.

"You don't want 'The Daily News' to display your picture as the Ferry Captain of Vice, do you, sir? Consider the Mann Act," I raised my voice. "Those men in the Packard have two young women, one white and one colored!"

As soon as I'd finished the sentence, Capt. Murphy signaled to one of the crew, who dashed out of the pilot house and down to the main deck. I said nothing more about this law that prohibited interstate trafficking with underaged women--a law used against Jack Johnson, the black heavyweight champ, when he married a white woman, way back at the beginning of the century. This may have been the only time the Mann Act came to the aid of my own race of people. I felt a momentary thrill at the power of law, normally for me a collection of words, words, words.

Meanwhile, another crewman left the cabin to check on the first. Both returned almost immediately.

"Canvas nothing," said the first, breathing heavily. "There are two women sitting up in the back seat, talking with the two men up front."

Capt. Murphy turned accusingly to me.

"Is one of the men colored?" I asked.

"Yeah."

"Is one of the women colored?"

"Yeah."

"What is a white man and a black man doing with a white woman and a colored girl?" I demanded, not knowing at first exactly what I meant except to indicate a lack of consistency in the mixing, some irregularity suggestive of illegal sexual activity. "Is the white woman a bleach-blonde?" That detail moved the suggestion even further into the world of crime. I admit with shame that my intention, as I realized, was to create the idea of prostitution in the minds of the captain and his crew. Desperation has its allowances; and this was no time to dilly-dally over fine points. The women, I promised myself, would never know. I made Glove promise, too, never to tell. He had a surprised look of rascality on his face. As for Capt. Murphy and his crew, this hint of sexual impropriety wasn't lost on them. They all got wild-eyed when they heard the phrase "bleach-blonde."

The captain and the other six jostled each other in a jumbled rush for the cabin door, anxious to see the women of dubious morality, especially the bleach-blonde Mrs. Belsberger. Primarily, of course, their purpose was to question the men, that is, their pimps. With the captain signaling for us to follow,

Glove and I rose and did as commanded, but not before I grabbed Thompson's pistol from the cabinet top where the captain had laid it. However, after descending to the main deck, we all found the Packard empty and its doors locked. Frustrated with the mystery getting so complicated, Capt. Murphy shouted an order for us, along with the six crewmen, to fan out and find the four missing people. I began to feel redeemed; but how the crew was supposed to accomplish the task presented another mystery, since only two of them could possibly recognize the missing four! Surely, they were still on the ferry, mingled among the passengers, themselves both black and white, or hidden in an obscure nook under capture on one deck or another. At least Herman and I were sure of what they looked like!

Evidently troubled by the same question, Capt. Murphy found a solution. He climbed the stairs to his cabin and made the following announcement:

"Will the driver of the gray Packard in the bow report to the pilot house immediately?" That was not a request but a command. The captain repeated the order several times, adding, "No passenger will be allowed to disembark until we see that man!"

Simple and naive, the announcement nevertheless had an effect. Nearly every passenger gathered towards the Packard to gawk at and chatter about it. Some stayed above to lean over the railing and do the same. The rest of the passengers came down to join the others on the main deck, amazing themselves at the sight of this automobile. This reaction of the crowd, unexpected as it was, proved helpful in isolating the two women and their abductors, who kept them hidden somewhere in a desperate effort to avoid notice and therefore capture. There were several minutes of unsettled calm as we entered the 42nd Street slip. Then amidst the squeaking and bumpity-bump of the ferry against the piles and the flapping of the seagulls rising from their perches, the man we'd all forgotten about, Wyatt Belsberger, emerged from his obscurity. It was as if the Devil himself had risen from a dark place in hell. Belsberger seemed larger than life, his slickly parted black hair blowing above his scalp like two horns and his eyes wild with excitement. He appeared on the main deck, shouting and waving, then running up the stairs to the second deck and then up to the pilot house, where Capt. Murphy met him.

The two men gestured to each other and yelled, but their words were mere sounds to us on the main deck. If my guess was correct, Belsberger identified himself as the owner of the vehicle, offering to bring the captain down to the bow, open the car door, and show his registration. He seemed to be denying that he knew of anyone else riding in the car! Then the two men descended the metal staircase, making for the Packard. As they pushed through the crowd on the lower deck, Wyatt caught my eye with his: that same strange, desperate look I saw in Kansas City--menacing this time, penetrating me with his darkness. I stared back as he pushed his oily hair back on either side. I felt his power; but I had no time to be afraid.

Now he and Capt. Murphy opened the car doors on both sides and got in. At this moment the passengers broke into applause; however, I deciphered Wyatt's intent. He wanted to distract the captain, who would then allow the passengers to disembark; and then Jamesetta and Barbara could be led onto the ramp and then onto the city streets while Capt. Murphy occupied himself in the car. The women would be led off separately, and in the racially-mixed crowd pouring off the ferry, nobody would notice anything peculiar.

Now, here is where my game-strategy came into play-- and caused me trouble with Jamesetta later on. If the two women had been separated, each guarded by a different thug, who should I help free first: the black lady or the bleach-blonde, each a lover of Buster Fenton? I decided in favor of Barbara Belsberger; and I'll say why shortly. Secondly, it would be necessary to trap Wyatt Belsberger at the same time; and that is when I told Herman to join Capt. Murphy and Wyatt inside the Packard, or at least hold them up there. The henchmen could get away, for all I cared; it would be better if they ran, in fact, since then they'd cause less harm. Finally, I wanted to save Jamesetta, and this maneuver offered the biggest challenge.

"Be careful, Herm," I said; "Belsberger is probably armed. If he has a gun in his hand, you stay clear, dig?"

He dug.

At this point, after reviewing all the aspects of the situation, I had to move into serious action.

I'd climbed halfway up the staircase toward the foot-passenger deck, when suddenly I spied Jimmy, her eyes rolling around, searching the crowd for me, as she strutted stiffly towards the ramp--with Leon the Spiker behind her, no doubt with a knife at her back. Now she saw me but couldn't wave, though I waved to her. I even smiled. To assure her that all would be well. But where was Barbara? She was my one trustworthy eye-witness, and even if her testimony couldn't be used in open court, it might nonetheless produce enough heat to get a confession from her husband or more testimony from his goons once they were caught. Now I saw her, too, among the cars, held in the rear of the crowd leaving the ferry. Perhaps Belsberger's plan was to keep her there till the last minute and then get her into his automobile as the ramp cleared; and then speed away. He could pick Jamesetta up later.

A thought I'd had about Wyatt was that he'd have been better off packing up and going back to Missouri instead of exercising his muscle trying to cover his tracks. But he was into the flow and couldn't stop. And now he was visible: too late for him to go anywhere.

Not even off the ferry. Curiosity lingered among the passengers, who continued to crush themselves around the Packard, so that Herman got pushed into the car when he approached, while the crew stood outside, flapping their arms in frustration. The mob closed in on the car like bees around a hive, and the horns of the other automobiles began to blare in a crazy rhythm, and only two cars up front were able to leave the ferry. This whole mess left Barbara and the white thug isolated. I saw her pulled backward through the aisle between the cars, towards the stern. That's when I made my move. I ran the rest of the way up the stairs, onto the second deck, across the side walkway, and then down in the rear, just as the two, Barbara and her captor, made their way to that point on the lower deck. Surprised, the hoodlum raised his knife, and Barbara broke free, running down towards the bow.

"Get that blonde!" I shouted, grappling with the thug: I couldn't let Barbara escape; I hoped one of the crew would stop her. There were a few among them whose eyes lit up when I referred to her earlier: There are reasons, both good and bad, that a man might want to intercept the flight of a morally dubious peroxide blonde!

I shouted, while the guy swiped at me with his knife; then again and again, as I danced out of the way, trying to grab his knife-hand and trip him backward with my foot. But not soon enough: The sonofabitch got me in the right shoulder, a good inch or two deep. I kicked him in the groin; he doubled over, but then with great effort he straightened up and leapt over the stern gate and into the water. I staggered up behind Barbara, whose forward progress ended with the crowd around the Packard. Two crewmen who heard my call were ready at hand.

"Hold that woman," I ordered them, and they did.

Now for Jimmy. Although the cars were still stalled, more and more people began to walk hastily off the ferry and up the ramp. Soon most of the passengers had proceeded outward, and the ramp was near cleared for the oncoming folks, who'd gathered at the upper end of it. I saw Jimmy now at the far end of the ramp about to enter the terminal with that ugly Leon. I paused in fatigue; I was out of breath, and my right shoulder continued to bleed. I went momentarily blank. What to do? What to do? Then I remembered that I was indeed Carl Slyder, the black baseball player with a moonbeam in his pocket. What could I not accomplish against the odds?

"Blood!" I began to shout. "Blood! Blood! Make way! Blood!"

As nobody likes somebody else's blood on them, the oncoming crowd quickly retreated up into the passenger holding-lane; while the exiting crowd, curious about the ruckus now coming off the ferry, pushed back out of the terminal to see the action! If there was blood, they wanted to see whose! Well, they pushed both Jamesetta and Leon with them. Leon turned full, then, to face me. Automatically, I showed my pistol, thinking what I don't know, that maybe he'd drop his shiv and run away. Bad thinking. The crowd reacted with an "Ohhh!" A few women screamed. I looked at the gun in my hand. I remembered the Sullivan Law, very strict in its penalty for carrying an unlicensed pistol. Even worse, I knew that a firearm was dangerous to use in a crowd or even aimed at a pair of people, one of them being innocent. Still, the crisis called for swift and risky action; and I was prepared to act riskily to save the girl. I had to do something really clever now, but what?

Normally, I would've rushed at Leon, while yelling at Jamesetta to escape; but my ankle ached grievously and I'd begun to limp, losing my nimbleness from too much chasing and twisting and whatnot. So there we were, Leon holding Jimmy with one hand and brandishing a knife in the other. A big knife, as I judged from its glinting at Jimmy's back fifty feet away. And here I was, one limping, bleeding black would-be detective, a disciple of Satchel Paige's theory of flow motion, flashing a little silver pistol, fully loaded--with the scared eyes of a sweating horse! I hoped someone might have sense enough to call for a cop.

But then I had an idea.

"Jamesetta!" I shouted. "Come back, baby! I love you! Come back, baby! You see how I bleed for you! Baby! Come back, or I will shoot myself!" This was, as Satchel would have it, the negative ploy.

Gripping it in my left hand, I put Thompson's pistol to my temple. The crowd went "Oooh!" like one person. Even Leon the Spiker seemed shocked. He stood still at the far end of the ramp, awaiting my next move.

"I have a gu-u-un!" I sang out, and then I proceeded as if it were the commencement of a blues lament. "Ple-e-ase, baby, come back to me! That Leon, he no go-o-od. No good at a-a-all. You got to leave that Le-e-on! You got to come back to me-e-e-e, baby! I said me-e-e-e! Or I swear, I swear I will sho-o-ot myself! I will shoot myself dead away-ay!" How did I ever think of this? Better yet, the crowd all turned to look at Leon.

He realized how vulnerable he was, and in the moment it took him to recover from his startlement, Jimmy freed herself, raced down the ramp, and put her arm around my waist. Leon, remembering that he ought to kill someone, decided to go for all or nothing. He came down the ramp after me--or her. I stiffened my arm and pointed at him; but luckily I had no need to shoot, for suddenly I heard the whining cry of a police siren. I saw the crowd of people in motion; I heard shouts and murmuring. Then I swiveled my head to look at Jimmy and fainted dead away.

185

CHAPTER TWELVE

"Brief Glory"

I awoke in Harlem Hospital. I'd taken a few stitches in my right shoulder, which ached under the bandages. The clearer I got the more it ached. I got so clear that after a few days of lying in the hospital I realized my playing days were at an end. What with a damaged throwing muscle and my already-twisted ankle, I'd never run as fast or swing a bat as well or throw as straight or reach down as easily to pick up a ground ball--never again. Maybe I could coach or even manage a team, but my glory run on the gritty diamond under the bright summer sun was over. Then I lay brooding over the events of the past weeks and figuring how the bad parts might've been avoided. Bad parts? Were there any good ones?

Pondering my fate, I wondered how I got into the hospital; I wondered what happened to Leon as he charged with his knife; and I wondered how Jamesetta fared standing next to me.

The girl came to visit on my third day in the hospital. She'd been busy with the investigation: held for questioning along with Barbara Belsberger, both at first considered to be prostitutes! Fortunately that ended well, though I blamed myself for starting everyone thinking they were. Moreover, and with great relief, I learned that she'd escaped the ferry incident without injury. What's more, she was eager to relate to me what transpired after I'd fainted.

Here was the picture. It seems Leon, distracted by the faces in the crowd and then the ambulance's siren, paid no attention to the uneven treading of the ramp. As a result, he tripped when his toe hit a metal ridge; and he fell, stumbling forward. His arm twisted under him, and his knife sliced into his neck when he hit the ferry's metal deck. He lay there, holding his neck and screaming as he bled, so Jimmy phrased it, like a stuck pig. At the same moment Jamesetta had the presence of mind to take Thompson's gun from my grasp and fling it into the water, hoping it would disappear into the oozy bottom and never be found again. Within seconds, the police arrived and arrested her, Barbara, Herman Glove (still sitting in the Packard), and Wyatt Belsberger (also in the car). I was loaded into the ambulance and brought here.

Thanks to Capt. Murphy, neither she nor Barbara had to spend the night in jail but were allowed to explain the complicated story in full.

"I hope you've been reading that," said Jimmy, indicating the Bible on my nightstand. A Bible? How did that get there? She didn't know, guessing that its presence was a standard gift of the hospital. That seemed odd, so I asked the nurse as she came to check my temperature, and she told me that Capt. Murphy had been in to visit me two days ago and left it for me, with instructions to read the dedication. The captain told her that this Bible was his personal one, accompanying him on all his trips back and forth on the ferry.

The dedication, to me, read: "'He who hath the steerage of my course, direct my sail!'" William Shakespeare.' Both Jimmy and I marveled at the sentiment.

She didn't have much to say after this, except to express relief at Wyatt's arrest. In her half-hour visit, she seemed tired and distant after telling her story, begging away with the excuse that she was needed at her job in Philadelphia, her vacation being over. So much for saving someone's life. She left me in a weary mood, depressed and lonely. So little gained for all that trouble. My shoulder ached something fierce now. I allowed that dark cloud of no-more-baseball to sink like a weight into my heart. I couldn't even browse through the reading material the girl had brought me, copies of "Life" magazine and "The Saturday Evening Post." A reward for the capture of Wyatt Belsberger might've eased my pain--a hundred dollars would've gotten a smile from me--but there was no reward. Would Barbara Belsberger offer me a gift of gratitude? I wondered. Hardly worth considering. Bad as he was, Wyatt was her husband!

Barbara came to visit me, too, after four days. The nurse had begun to prepare me for release, changing my

187

bandages and giving me instructions on bathing the wound. But Barbara barged right in with a copy of "The Amsterdam News," speaking in and around the nurse's ministrations. She was excited over the front page headline: ATHLETE'S KILLER NABBED. Underneath appeared a photo of Buster in suit and tie, though I wished it had been in a Bluebird uniform. I showed up on page three, laid out unconscious on an ambulance cot, ready to be hauled off to Harlem Hospital.

"You're a hero," Barbara exclaimed, "and now the world knows it."

I nodded in appreciation.

"You could smile," she said.

"Thank you," I replied, halfway between a grimace and a grin.

When the nurse left, Barbara kissed me on the forehead. "Thank you," she said. "Those bums could've gotten us all killed. I'll always believe you saved my life."

I nodded in appreciation.

"I know also," she continued, "that you deserve a big monetary reward. At least a thousand dollars. Unfortunately, my money is going to be tied up for a while, or I'd take care of that. But wait until my divorce. That's a promise."

"I could use a job," I commented.

"Really?"

I explained about the long-term effects of my injuries.

"I may know somebody," she said. "Let me look into it. Would you mind relocating to San Juan, Puerto Rico?"

I shrugged. Ow. My shoulder. I couldn't even shrug properly. The person I think she had in mind was an agent for the players in the Caribbean, a guy named Sanchez. A shifty character. He lived summers in Chicago.

"Oh, really," she said when she saw my mood. "Your condition isn't all that bad. Why don't you and Jamesetta join me for dinner next week in Chinatown? She'll be back in New York. Monday's her day off."

Chinatown? That was interesting. I was leaving the hospital today, so what the hell. I accepted. Anyway, I needed to hear what Jamesetta had to say for herself in a more personal way.

"But what about Aunt Monique, Jamesetta's aunt? The one Jamesetta visits when she comes to Harlem?"

"Of course," answered Barbara, who I'd concluded was pretty good-natured even if she was a bleach-blonde who'd gotten Buster killed.

I'll interrupt myself to mention that Aunt Monique had paid me a visit several days earlier. She came when I was either delirious or under medication. She wrung her little hands and worried about my deliverance from evil, as she put it; and muttered, "Too bad, too bad." Beyond that I could barely comprehend her, though I spoke a few words groggily. Then the nurse persuaded her to leave.

Now, as Barbara talked away, a gentleman in a tan suit entered my room, a handsome, dapper fellow with a neat mustache and dark brown wavy hair. Of all the people I'd met on this adventure he had the smoothest and most confident step. No athlete I knew moved so effortlessly and so directly. When he reached forward to shake my hand, I supposed it was some Latin lawyer--some Cuban, perhaps--come to take my case to court, suing the State of New York or New Jersey for what happened on the 42nd Street Ferry.

"Let me introduce myself, Moonbeam," he said; "I'm the Rev. Adam Clayton Powell, Jr. of the Abyssinian Baptist Church on 138th Street here in Harlem."

My jaw must've dropped quite literally as I stared at this man's face. Here was the white minister--so he struck me at the time--I'd viewed outside the church when I went to pick up Jamesetta before our trip to Brooklyn! That day I could identify him as the Rev. Powell at a distance but not today and not close up, not in my disoriented state! He certainly surprised me.

"There are many colors of the Negro race," he said when he noticed my reaction, "and mine is one of them. Just as we have many colors, we have many talents, many strengths and virtues. You, Moonbeam, are a man who personifies those racial attributes. That's why I've come here today to shake

189

your hand." So he did, again. As he did, I saw flashing lights. They popped white flashes several times before I understood that my photograph was being taken, together with the Rev. Powell and Barbara Belsberger. Oh, there were a good ten to fifteen shots more, with a variety of poses, alone and with others.

"That was my little speech," said the Rev. Powell as he sat down next to me. His manner became relaxed and confidential. "That was for the record, Moonbeam." When he saw my perplexity, he explained: "For 'Ebony' magazine. They're doing a photo feature on the man who caught the killer of Buster Fenton. That's you, man. In another few months, when this edition comes out, you'll be famous. Everyone will know the hero, Moonbeam Slyder, second baseman for the Jersey City Bluebirds. More people will know you than ever they knew your teammate Buster Fenton. Now, you just lie there and think about that."

"I'm a bit dazed, Reverend," I began. "I don't know whether I'm a hero or whether anyone besides a few friends and family members will remember me for anything. I did steal home once on Satchel Paige."

The Rev. Powell laughed. He called over the photographer, who worked also as feature editor for "Ebony," and introduced him as Philip Doughty.

"I have to leave, Moonbeam, but my friend Mr. Doughty will stay behind with you for a little chat. He has questions to ask. You tell him the whole story with all the gory details. He'll write it up fine." He rose and left.

"Thank you, Congressman," said Philip Doughty.

"Thank you," Mr. Adam Clayton Powell, Jr. called back from the hall. He moved fast. And "Congressman"! Well, well, I had made progress in the world. The visit of New York City's first person of African descent elected to the United States House of Representatives proved something that way, though I suspected that if my fame were as short-lived as his visit I wouldn't stand to improve my lot by much. Still, Congressman! Now "Ebony"! Just before, a kiss on the forehead from the glamorously blonde Barbara Belsberger!

Wouldn't Herman Glove be green as a ripe watermelon with envy!

During the interview I made sure to mention him and Jamesetta Kelly as two key operators in the criminals' capture. "Jamesetta Kelly," I emphasized, "you should be photographing her. She's the beautiful one." I believe I meant those words when I said them, groggy as I was.

When the journalist left, I began fretting about Jimmy's not being here--about her being back down in Philadelphia working as a chambermaid. Some chambermaid. I regretted how she'd missed her opportunity for nationwide attention and how she deserved to be seen in "Ebony" as much as any American girl in any American magazine. I couldn't think of anyone more appealing, what with her dimpled cheeks and bright brown eyes! What with her bravery in the face of danger! Her quick reflexes and her steadfast loyalty! But then I questioned why when she visited me she'd been so abrupt. Was she all right herself? Had she really returned to Philly? Or was her loyal nature drawn back to reminiscing about Buster? And changing her mind about being angry with him. I worried that she'd come to the conclusion that Buster, even in his grave, was her one true love and never me, yeah, poor me, lying here, half crippled on a hospital bed in Harlem. Women are, after all, strange and inconstant creatures, I reasoned, and her loyalty to Buster could only mean for her to forget about me! Why else did she leave me lonesome here, brooding and brooding about her?

I shouldn't have rushed her. That's what I told myself. I shouldn't have gotten her so deeply involved. I shouldn't have exposed her to danger.

Or maybe she was just a moody thing: happy one hour and miserable the next. Not a good recommendation for a long and loving relationship!

My mind wandered to my ex-wife and what I might've done to keep her; but now she seemed not so vivid as during those times when I'd be blue and imagining her in our better days. My heart felt no heaviness over her loss--and, recently, no bitterness. I'd come to a position of neutrality regarding her. Now, when I came out of my reverie, I realized I'd had a sad, quiet smile on my face.

And there was Barbara Belsberger smiling back at me. She hadn't left.

"Back with us, Moonbeam?" she asked.

Apparently, I'd gone off in a kind of daydream that slipped into a short doze.

Now Barbara, who'd joined me in the interview, filling in episodes and minor details from her own eventful experience, stayed behind when she saw me fading out. She assured me that Jamesetta would join us Monday at the Canton Sun and Moon Restaurant in Chinatown. Ah, yes, I remembered. She further assured me that Jimmy wasn't entirely in grief, certainly no deep grief for Buster, not since she herself, Barbara, had come on the scene and confirmed Jamesetta's worst expectations in Buster, as she faced the other woman in his life. Then she urged me to say something nice to Jamesetta and not behave so professionally. Professionally?

"You know," Barbara explained, "Keeping it platonic. Always at work."

What did she mean by that phrase "platonic"? Or was that Jamesetta's word? Here, all along, I thought I'd been too aggressive. Well, maybe I'd been too careful, worrying about being too aggressive. Maybe I could've been, what, passionate? But when? When did I have time for pitching woo with a newly-made widow-fiancée and my shuttling back and forth over the river and my victimization by hoodlums in Harlem and elsewhere? Hadn't she herself made the solution of the crime her top priority? Hadn't she joined me in that? Right. So that was me, huh, always at work? Women. You say salt, and they say pepper. And never shall those twain meet.

Stewing over Jamesetta's attitude, I speculated on others who treated me casually, who never even came to see me. Such as Toby Hughes. Hadn't he heard? Barbara shrugged. Or the others on the team. Glove, especially. I knew he read "The Amsterdam News." Where the devil was he? Barbara knew nothing about the team, but she suspected that Herman Glove might've been arrested at the ferry. He might still be in custody in a local lock-up.

"Have you got a lawyer, Mrs. Belsberger," I asked. "A New York lawyer?"

She had.

"Could I ask you to check into the whereabouts of Herman Glove?"

I could, and she would. As Barbara helped lead me down to the hospital lobby, we stopped there to telephone her lawyer. This fellow agreed to ask around. He'd leave a message at the reception desk in the Waldorf, where I would rest up at Barbara's expense until we sprung Glove. She herself had no problem staying in New York, now that her husband was in prison awaiting another bail hearing. At the initial one, the judge expressed fear over Wyatt's setting sail for England in October, he and Barbara having purchased tickets in high publicity; so the man was safe in jail for a while, needing to prove that if he were granted bail he wouldn't leave the country to avoid trial.

One more thing in the hospital: the bill came to eighty-five dollars! That amount, however, I didn't have to pay since "Ebony" magazine, I was told, had voluntarily picked up the tab! I wondered what other publication might want to give me an interview.

I won't describe the ins and outs of springing Glove from the 5th District Jail. After all the rigamarole, after the white lawyer threw up his hands, saying he'd checked everywhere without a clue, Barbara'd made a last desperate call to the Rev. Powell, who managed to end Herman's brief incarceration. Seems the problem was Herman's last name: It wasn't Glove; it was Anderson! How do you like that? I got to rib him over that one. Herman explained later that about twenty years back, he'd made a few great plays at home plate on some amateur team in Pittsburgh and everyone started calling him Glove. He was young and proud, and he decided to go with it. But legally he was Anderson. "Northern European roots, after all," Toby scoffed, laughing, when he heard this. Well, he'd stay Glove to me, but he was angry at first for having spent almost a week behind bars; however, when he saw the wound in my shoulder and then read the article in "The Amsterdam News" and then heard about my conversation with the "Ebony" journalist, he could barely hold himself in!

"We're heroes, man!" he shouted. "You and me, we're heroes. We're as famous as Joe Louis! Forget that. Hell, I'm calling you Douglas MacArthur, and you can call me General Ike!"

Believe it or not, we found Herman's Chrysler parked not far from the 42nd Street dock in Hell's Kitchen. Sometimes rough neighborhoods are so rough nobody touches the obvious stuff. We got in and took the ferry over to Weehawken and then down to Jersey City to see Toby. This wasn't the "Niagara," Capt. Murphy's boat, or else we'd have stopped up in the pilot house to pay our respects. That would be for another time.

As we anticipated, Toby acted angrily. Well, he didn't act; he'd been unaware of our involvement in the ferry incident, of which he'd never heard a word. All he remembered was that I'd run off the field for no sensible reason and that Glove caught the fever and followed me. We'd left him in the lurch. But only for a week. He hadn't read the Harlem newspaper, but when we showed him the headline and the article with the photos and the business with Wyatt Belsberger, his eyes showed more white than a boiled egg. There was my body being loaded into an ambulance, and there were Glove's name and my name on page three! Then we spoke of Glove's incarceration in the 5th District Jail: That touched Toby in the joy spot. He laughed until he doubled over. He said that Herman should have felt right at home in prison since he'd already spent half his life behind the bars of his catcher's mask!

"And I thought you boys had run off and joined the Marines!" He enjoyed our adventure no end.

I left Glove with Toby, planning to rest a bit at my rooming house. I left, but not before getting a promise from Toby that in spite of our mishaps we'd still have jobs with the Bluebirds. Toby replied that I'd better heal fast, because there was nothing he could do for an unhealed heel. He was so glad to see us, I guessed, that he couldn't stop cracking silly jokes. He went on to quote Shakespeare's "Hamlet" about "to be or not to be"--meaning my job--but he made it sound like his own name, so that it came out, "Tobee or not Tobee": signifying that I'd have to cotton to his rules more seriously. He added he'd contact the Negro paper in Jersey City to make sure they had the story of our greatness. Our reception by that newspaper depended on "Tobee or not Tobee," as he repeated and continued to laugh at his own joke. Somehow he'd worked his way into the act.

"You be the man, Tobee; you be the man," I said, laughing along with him.

Next day I rested in bed, lying about, arranging the details of my room and recalling the events that began with Buster's joining the team in late June. He had us knocking at the league championship door. But now the baseball season was three-quarters done, and the Bluebirds had sunk into fourth place. So our glory was diminished by Buster's passing; yet ironically mine had taken its short flight because of it. Herman's too. Who'd ever think that Herman Glove would achieve celebrity, however brief?

I missed Buster, though. I tried one more time to find out his real name. I asked Barbara about it, but she was dumbfounded as the rest. I called the operator to ask for Buster's parents' phone number, only to be told that the Fentons had no listing. I told myself that I'd check the gravestone in the cemetery in six months; but then I let that go and never did.

He had his contradictions, this Buster, but overall he was one outstanding young man. He hoped to fly higher than the rest of us, with a white woman and in the white leagues. But he was obliged to make a choice, the wrong choice, as I saw it, and that cut him down as he stretched his wings and made for the unreachable blue. He couldn't have his cake and eat it too. Still, he died young, untarnished; his brief candle shone brightly, and he'd always be remembered in that light--at least by a few--but never, I came to believe, by his rightful name. He wouldn't enjoy the glory of a Robinson or a Doby or a Paige or even a Hank Thompson, cheered on by fans of all colors in the Major League ballparks of these United States. In a sense, then, as I reflected later, his flight resembled the destiny of those many fine athletes in the Negro Leagues, whose performances, whose talents, whose game-ness, brought them just so far out of obscurity and into the faint fame of black baseball--and then abandoned them on the edge of the horizon, less recognized than their privileged, lighter-skinned brothers, less glamorized, less appreciated by sport fans; and so, in a sense, less a part of the game; on the edge of the horizon, see, as the sun set now on that moment in American sports, casting the Negro Leagues forever into twilight.

Somewhere there must be a weighing of true worth that is just and eternal. But what mortal knows who holds the scales and where they are kept? That, as Hamlet would say, is the question.

Best not to brood about those things. After all, for whatever reward might come, I'd succeeded in becoming more of myself, more a man of the world. Also, I was alive and lucky to be so. The white thug's knife had been aimed at my heart as I struggled with him. I'd feinted to the left and then to the right, just as I might've in an attempt to steal second base. He struck hard but failed to hit home. But I'd hurt my ankle again as we grappled; and that was the injury that would undo me in the long run. Even so, I had my picture in the newspaper and would soon have nationwide recognition from the article in "Ebony." How much glory does a man need? Some are born heroes, and some die heroes; and some heroes are made along the way: Essentially, though, a hero's divinity, if such it is, is better known to the Lord and Maker of Goodness, who lives beyond this mortal life.

Briefly, then, for the rest of the story. Once all the facts began to jibe, the New York District Attorney planned to indict Wyatt Belsberger for Buster Fenton's murder, but the charge was going to be Second Degree Manslaughter, and Wyatt would plead self-defense in a street fight over who had a right to his wife! Shortly afterward it came out that he was involved in an illegal gambling operation in Kansas City and would be standing trial there once he'd served his jail term in New York. So there'd be no electric chair for him, just eighteen months in Sing Sing with time off for good behavior--and then sixteen months in a pen in Missouri. I heard later that while he was in prison Barbara sued him for divorce, claiming half the potato chip operation. She took over for a while, then re-sold her share to someone who ruined the business, and Wyatt wound up broke. I wonder if he ever learned to control his violent temper.

As for Wyatt's henchmen, Leon the Spiker recovered from his throat wound but lost his voice permanently: He spent six years in Sing Sing, while the other thug, the guy who tried to kill me, escaped apprehension and punishment--he was the one, I will remind you, who cracked Buster's skull with a lead pipe: so Wyatt told his wife. I might also mention that Bumpy Johnson, in matters unrelated to this case, also went on to spend time in prisons upstate New York. So much for his own employment.

I'd see Tom Baird again, usually when the Bluebirds played the Monarchs; but we never spoke, although he'd nod to me when he caught my eye.

For his part, he stayed active in black ball until the end, supporting his players in their efforts to make a dollar through the 1950s. He was basically a decent fellow, mistakenly judging his friend as he judged himself, not comprehending the evil side to Belsberger's character until too late. Secretly, though, as it came out later, both he and Wyatt were registered in the Kansas KKK! But that was earlier in the century; and he expressed regrets about that membership. Yet it was this, I realized, that rattled a fear in me--it is still a mystery to me why --this ability of his to choose wrongly and freely, even though he had a strength for goodness, being wrong and unpunished, that is, merely because he was white.

After signing with the St. Louis Brown's, Hank Thompson achieved the distinction of playing ball with the New York Giants in 1948, providing Horace Stoneham with a long-ball hitter for five or six good seasons. Hank forgave me the loss of his little silver pistol once he read my story in "Ebony." He refused compensation when I offered to pay for it. He must've had another gun in reserve, though, because he went and got himself arrested sometime later, in a shooting incident in a hole-in-the-wall saloon, which left another man dead. There's no telling where a man's wayward self will lead him. Fortunately, with Mr. Stoneham's help Hank managed to clear himself of a murder rap, claiming self-defense. Then he went on to some pretty respectable years in the National League.

After our dinner at the Canton Sun and Moon, I lost track of Barbara Belsberger. She promised to stay in touch but never did, except once, and that was three years later to write of her divorce, enclosing a check for one thousand dollars, "For Heroism," as she phrased it. She was unusual in her way, allowing herself to be bullied by a misfit like Wyatt (a man out of his league in a few categories), on the one hand, and then having the courage to take up publicly with Buster, on the other. As to her fate, I heard bits of gossip now and then from KC players. One was that she married a left-handed Mexican pitcher and lived with him south of the border in Monterrey. Another was that she reunited with Belsberger after his release from prison in Missouri in 1949. The third was that she'd appeared in Senegal as the wife of a black French-speaking prince of some tribe with an unpronounceable name. The woman had exotic tastes, I believe, but I saw her as conventional, too: witness her need to find her beauty in being blonde. As to her true destiny, however, I will let you come to your own conclusion.

Herman Glove and I became friends at last. We'd known each other for five years, and it took finally one ferry ride to open our minds to the other's virtue. As a testament to this adjustment, I agreed that "Ebony" was a worthwhile magazine, and he said the same about "Life." He admitted that I was faster than Cool Papa Bell that 1946 season, and I complimented him on his loyalty and sense of commitment, which were better than mere speed, I said. We both stayed with the Bluebirds some five years longer, both as coaches; until I became manager after Toby suddenly died during the last half of the '51 season. Then in another year the team just folded.

However, an interesting, although tragic, chance opened up new possibilities for us. Herman and I pursued full-time what had been a growing sideline, a partnership in the field of private investigation, with a specialty in sporting world cases. But that's another story.

Our dinner that Monday night in Chinatown began as a quiet affair. Both women had been to the beauty parlor, and both were stunning. Barbara had a new hairdo, her long blond tresses draping her shoulders and cutting across one eyebrow in the front, like Veronica Lake's. Jamesetta's do was perfect, a glossy black curling-up under her chin with a straight part down one side. The two made me feel ungroomed. I touched my own side-part to reassure myself it hadn't grown in. The two wore black dresses with trim white-lace collars, and again I didn't feel up to their elegance. I needed a new sports jacket and new shoes: I sat there ashamed of my jacket's bagginess and the scuffs on the tips of my shoes. Why didn't I cough up fifteen cents for a shine when I walked off the ferry? But here I was, facing two extraordinary women, twins almost in a black-and-white way. Life had its moments, and so I stopped feeling negative about myself. No other man in the restaurant had such gorgeous company.

Aunt Monique declined to join us, pleading her need to rest for work the next day. I promised myself to have her out to dine on the weekend--or to bring an order of delicatessen food to the apartment for her and me to lunch on. Of course, I still remembered about pledging to take her and Jamesetta to the Apollo: but the niece had made all that complicated, for the moment. I wanted to ask after her aunt, but Jamesetta acted so strangely quiet, I was distracted simply by watching her eat. Almost as if in pantomime, she munched on her egg roll, sipped her wonton soup, and started eating her lobster Cantonese, touching the creamed lobster pieces so daintily I thought she'd spent the last few days at a refresher course in charm school. Pleasant but distant, she smiled noncommittally at whatever Barbara or I said to her. Just as the dessert course came; for Barbara insisted that we all order ice cream specials, with whipped cream, nuts, and chocolate syrup; our blonde friend excused herself and disappeared in the direction of the ladies' room. She never returned. Just two ice cream specials appeared on our table. Looking at these and waiting, I was forced to break the embarrassed silence.

"What's the problem," I asked. "Did you and she have a fight?"

Jamesetta shook her head no.

"You feeling kind of sick?" I questioned.

Another no.

"Well, then, come on: Tell me what," I insisted.

She breathed deeply as she brought herself up in the seat. She looked ceilingward and then straight at me.

"You," she said carefully, "have disappointed me."

"I have?"

"Yes."

"How?"

She paused, then patted the edges of her mouth with her large white napkin.

"I don't want you to think I'm vain or self-centered," she began, then paused slightly. "But everyone heard."

"What?"

"You rescued her first."

"I did?" Frankly, I barely recalled.

"You did."

"And how did you discover that?

"She told me and everyone else."

"You and everyone else?"

"She told the police, and I and everyone else overheard."

"Well, I'll be damned," I said. She blinked. I'd never used strong language with her.

I wiped my mouth with the large white napkin. I sipped cold water. I apologized for her misunderstanding of my actions on the ferry. As it all came back to me, I explained about tactics and strategy, how we won the war in Europe and the Pacific and how in the same way I succeeded in triumphing over Wyatt Belsberger on land and sea. Through strategy and tactics. She had to smile then. I described the scene of struggle in full, relating the sequence of my thoughts during the crisis, and how and why I chose to act as I did. I didn't, however, go into the theory of flow motion, since that seemed eccentric at the time.

"You were my first concern but the least of my worries," I said, "because between you, Barbara, and Herman Glove, I trusted you to make the most independent decisions."

"Meaning?"

"Meaning you were the smartest one in the least danger. Once Barbara was free and Wyatt surrounded in his Packard, the hoodlum's hold on you was weak. See? What could that ugly Leon have done?"

"Killed me."

"Or me. No, not in that crowd; and I was prepared to prevent him."

"By fainting," she smiled at last.

"Standing next to you."

"But he came at me or you or both of us with that big knife."

"Too bad he didn't watch his step," I added.

She kind of studied me.

"You were a hero," she said gently.

"Some hero," I replied.

She sipped her cold water. Then she changed the subject.

"Aunt Monique claims you have the sweetest smile," she said.

"I have many smiles," I answered. Then I told her of my Uncle Louis' comment about my big colored mouth.

"Aunt Monique," she said, "claims that a good, strong smile comes from the eyes."

"My eyes?"

"Yours, yes."

"I love your Aunt Monique."

She paused, glancing down at her ice cream sundae. The whipped cream topping had lost its puffiness. It was then I realized our friend was gone for the night; that she had, in fact, set us up to sit like this, face to face, over a white table cloth. It was then I realized, too, that Jamesetta, for all that I'd thought her plain, and perhaps attractive in her plainness, was nothing of the sort: she was a beauty--and she was so because of my feeling for her. In spite of everything.

"You think she was first in my heart?" I heard myself asking her.

She didn't reply.

"As you believe the case to have been with Buster?" I ventured.

She was stony, not looking up at me, looking instead at that stupid whipped cream topping slowly liquefying over the chocolate syrup and the ice cream.

"Not true," I said quietly. "And you know that. What kind of proof do you need?"

No answer. A few minutes elapsed. We rose together. I called the waiter, asking for the bill. He told me it had already been paid by the blonde lady. I gave him a dollar.

"You've disappointed me too," I said as we descended the stairs to street level.

"How so?" she wondered.

"By lying."

"About Buster?"

"And other things."

"Did you think I was perfect?" she asked.

"Not at all," I said; "to the contrary, and even worse when I heard your sarcasm."

"I see," she said.

"And you were not supposed to run off to Philadelphia that night with Barbara."

"Should I have waited for you to return?"

"Yes."

We came to the street-landing and walked out of the restaurant. On the sidewalk we stood turning our heads this way and that. It was getting dark earlier now, and here in Chinatown with its many colored lights, we needed a moment to orient ourselves. We stood, silently inhaling the cool summer night, momentarily dazed. There were no more words. We couldn't decide which way to go. In a second we each walked in the opposite direction, when I nearly bumped into an old, blind, sweet-faced Chinese lady selling roses. I bought one, then turned back to hand it to Jimmy as she, too, turned to face me. We saw only each other's eyes. Then, of course, we knew.

THE END

8983947R0

Made in the USA
Charleston, SC
31 July 2011